Sarah Edworthy

The Olympic Torch Relay

Follow the Flame of London 2012

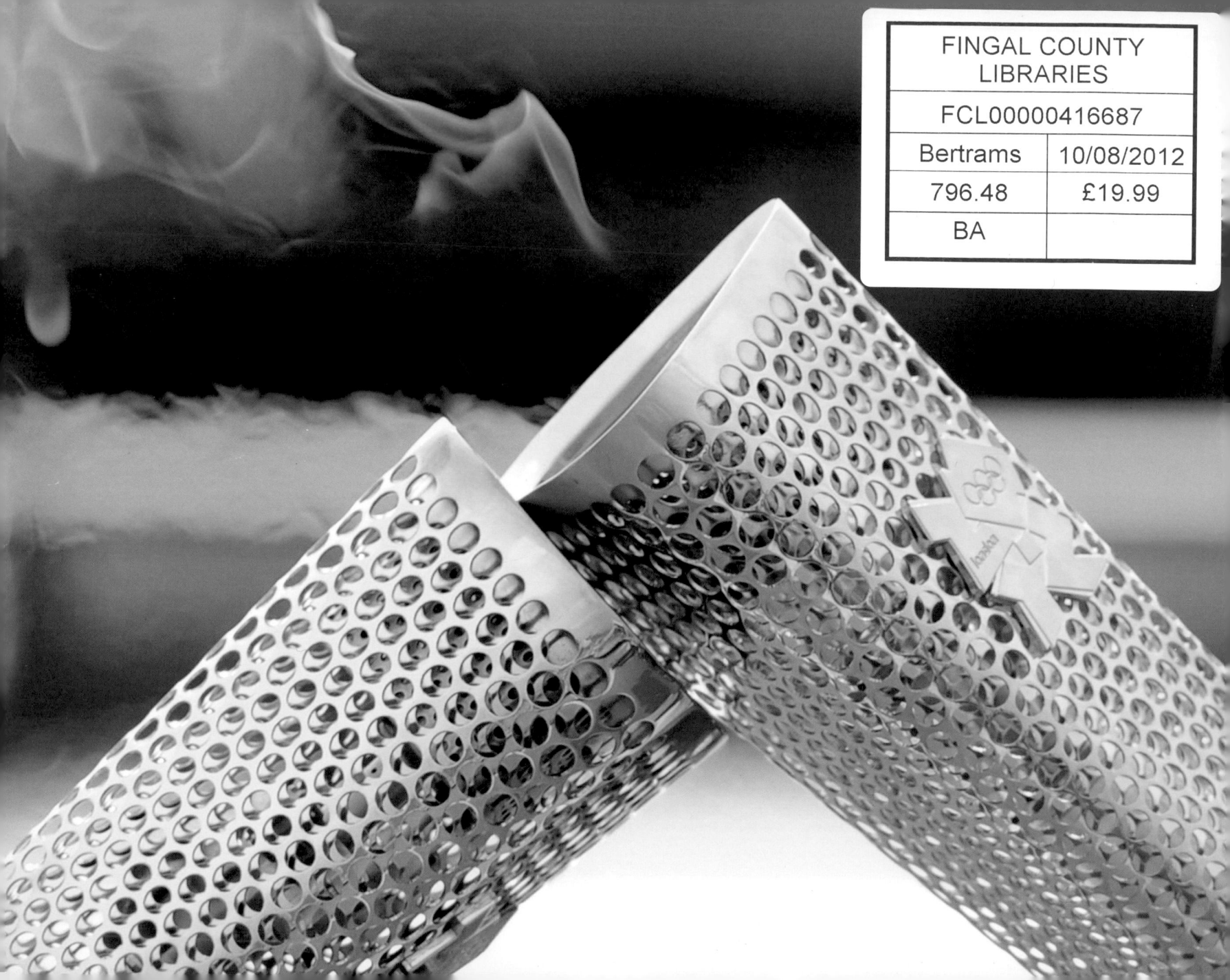

Sarah Edworthy

The Olympic Torch Relay

Follow the Flame of London 2012

This edition first published in 2012

Copyright © text Sarah Edworthy 2012

Registered office
John Wiley & Sons Ltd, The Atrium, Southern Gate,
Chichester, West Sussex, PO19 8SQ,
United Kingdom

An official London 2012 publication.

A catalogue record for this book is available from the British Library.

ISBN 978-1119-97315-7 (paperback);
ISBN 978-1119-94151-4 (ebk); 978-1119-97916-6 (ebk);
ISBN 978-1119-97917-3 (ebk); 978-1119-97918-0 (ebk)

Typeset in Futura

Design by Rawshock Design

Printed in the UK by Butler Tanner & Dennis

Contents

6 Foreword

8 Introduction

28 **Chapter 1**　19 to 25 May

56 **Chapter 2**　26 May to 1 June

80 **Chapter 3**　2 to 8 June

104 **Chapter 4**　9 to 15 June

130 **Chapter 5**　16 to 22 June

154 **Chapter 6**　23 to 29 June

178 **Chapter 7**　30 June to 6 July

202 **Chapter 8**　7 to 13 July

226 **Chapter 9**　14 to 20 July

250 **Chapter 10**　21 to 27 July

276 **Chapter 11**　As Night Falls…

286 Index

288 Acknowledgements

Foreword

I was extremely honoured to be asked to be the first Torchbearer of the London 2012 Olympic Torch Relay from Land's End. I grew up on the Helford River, near Falmouth, and race under the colours of The Royal Cornwall Yacht Club, so the invitation to carry the Flame in Cornwall was one I accepted proudly.

For 70 days, the Torch Relay truly fired the public imagination. Much more than a countdown to an exciting festival of sport, it was an event in itself – an amazing celebration of people and places along its 8,000-mile route. I'll never forget the buzz of anticipation from the crowd gathered around me as I stood by the Land's End signpost, just before 7am on 19 May, waiting for the helicopter to fly around the headland with the Olympic Flame on board. It was pretty surreal, wearing that official 001 Torchbearer badge and realising I was about to initiate the inspiring human chain that would take the Olympic Flame to all corners of the British Isles.

It was a beautiful, calm morning as the sun rose over the sea, but it was one of the more nervous moments of my life. For an athlete focused on success, the Olympic Flame symbolises the very spirit of the Olympic Games. It takes on a special significance at the Opening Ceremony when the Cauldron is lit. During the period prior to a Games, when the Torch Relay traditionally stokes up anticipation around a host nation, most athletes are still trying to qualify or win selection. My selection was confirmed last September, so I appreciated the opportunity to be involved in the Torch Relay and savour the build-up to my home Games.

I was blown away by the reaction. At 7.08am, when my Torch was pumping out a big Flame in the breeze, cameras clicked, people cheered, clapped and whistled. I didn't have any particular plan of action, I didn't know how fast I should run, but everyone was so excited I decided to walk. I wanted everyone to be part of it. People stretched hands out to touch the Torch; they held up babies to get a better glimpse of the Flame. I caught up with the Torch Relay later that day in Falmouth and was staggered by the number of people who turned out. It was unbelievable. I've never seen so many on the streets.

I saw for myself the collective pull of the Olympic Flame and all it symbolises. The fact that the majority of the Torchbearers were nominated by others for their inspirational qualities gave the event a remarkable emotional dynamic. To witness the fleeting glimpse of the Flame or party at the evening celebrations was truly a once-in-a-lifetime experience.

This book is a vibrant commemoration of a piece of history, when our streets came alive with patriotism, pride in our communities and fantastic support for our local heroes. In years to come, families can open it as a keepsake and remember the amazing day London 2012 came to their home town.

Ben Ainslie

Introduction

Dictionaries offer a number of definitions for the noun 'flame' [fleym]: 1. The condition of visible combustion; 2. A portion of ignited gas or vapour; 3. A glow or brilliant light; scintillating lustre; 4. Bright colouring; a streak or patch of colour; 5. Intense ardour, zeal, or passion; 6. A bright beam or ray of light from a heavenly body, celestial.

The Olympic Flame complies with all of the above, and its lighting never fails to spark an emotional response. The Lighting Ceremony, which follows the same ritual before every Winter and Summer Games, is choreographed to look as timeless as the values of peace, unity and friendship it symbolises. It is staged amid the ruins of the temple of Hera in the shade of Mount Kronos, close to the stadium that for a thousand years hosted the ancient Games in Greece. On 10 May 2012 Edward Barber and Jay Osgerby, designers of the London 2012 Olympic and Paralympic Torches, watched the mid-morning formalities with excitement, pride and the slight feeling they had stepped into a surrealist cameo. Never before had one of their creations been launched to a global audience attended by a host of 'priestesses' in flowing white robes. A Greek high priestess kindles the sacred Flame from the sun's rays with a parabolic mirror and the fire dances into life. There, in the burst of a flickering light, the stylish gold triangular Torch, conceived in Barber and Osgerby's Shoreditch studio, officially became the Flame's latest receptacle. Now it had to safeguard the sacred Flame en route to the Cauldron in the Olympic Stadium where it marked the official start of the Olympic Games. 'It was amazing to be in Olympia for the lighting of our Torch,' Barber recalls. 'After nearly two years spent hands-on developing it, we found it a very moving experience,' adds Osgerby.

The Torch, for all its elegance, needs to be robust, with the Olympic Flame's fragility a part of its enduring appeal. Even its lighting cannot be assumed: in 2000, prior to the Sydney Games, cloudy conditions caused the high priestess arm ache as she patiently held the Torch in position and waited in vain for the sun's rays to ignite it in the ceremonial mirror. In the end a Flame lit at the previous day's dress rehearsal, and reverently secured in a lantern as a contingency measure, came to the rescue.

The Olympic Flame is particularly emotive because it represents something that cannot be extinguished: a sense of looking forward and hopefulness. The Lighting Ceremony in Greece may be a modern amalgam of classical myths – and the Relay itself a 'tradition' developed in the modern era by the organisers of the Berlin 1936 Games – but in its reclaimed form the Olympic Torch Relay has become a powerful unifying event. Few would deny that society benefits from a biennial reminder of high ideals and noble sportsmanship. The Torch Relay, taking the form of a human chain, passing a force for good from person to person, stokes excitement and expectation for the world's biggest peacetime event, and restores a sense of optimism to those who experience it.

In 1948, the last time London hosted the Games, the Olympic Flame was seen as a beacon of hope, offering much-needed healing after the Second World War. London and other major British cities were still cratered with bombsites. Food and clothes were still rationed; petrol was in short supply. Thousands of families were making do in temporary housing, and everyone was eking out everyday essentials. In what became known as the Austerity Games, athletes from 58 nations were housed in RAF camps, schools and nurses' hostels, and had to bring their own towels. The British team were instructed to make their own uniforms. Billy Butlin, the holiday-camp owner, invited the athletics team to train at his camp in Clacton-on-Sea.

With some boldness, the Organising Committee led by Lord Burghley (winner of a gold medal at the Amsterdam 1928

Greek actress Ino Menegaki, acting as high priestess, passes the Olympic Flame to the first Torchbearer, British-born swimmer Spyros Gianniotis, on 10 May 2012, during the Lighting Ceremony at the ancient site of Olympia. The Olympic Flame was lit from the sun's rays using a parabolic mirror before being carried into the Panathinaiko Stadium.

Games) resolved to 'capture the imagination of the public and the spirit of the Olympic Torch' by continuing with the Relay format ratified by the International Olympic Committee two years before the Berlin 1936 Games. The London 1948 Games were to be a celebration of the post-war world emerging from victory; an event delivered on a shoestring to raise spirits and galvanise the nation to start building for the future. Indeed, George VI believed that the Games would help restore morale to a weary Britain and signal a return to 'normality' around the globe.

Operating within a tight budget, the British Olympic Committee commissioned Ralph Lavers, an architect with a background in Egyptian archaeology, to design an inexpensive Torch. It had to be easy to manufacture, 'of pleasing appearance and a good example of British craftsmanship'. Lavers' design was simple and classic: a robust stem capped by a cylindrical bowl. Cast in a hiduminium alloy known to retain strength at high temperatures, with a length of 47cm and a weight of 960g, it was adorned with an inscription in capital letters that read 'With thanks to the bearer' and with the Olympic Rings punched out on the bowl. Two types were made: one hiduminium, with hexamine/naphthalene tablets stacked up inside a perforated steel burner for the 1,416 Relay legs that were run across Europe and England; and another for the final stretch in the Stadium, where it would carry a magnesium Flame in a stainless steel holder to guarantee it could be seen even in bright daylight. The government's Fuel Research Station oversaw practicalities such as cost, materials, fuel and testing to ensure the robustness of the Flame. The testing process included carrying the lighted Torch out in a gale with heavy rain – typical English summer weather! – and touting it around on a warm fine day with a gentle breeze. The results of the trials were deemed satisfactory, and 1,688 Torches were duly packed and despatched.

The 'Relay of Peace' was admirably imaginative in concept considering the rawness of post-war Europe. On its way from the Peloponnese to Wembley, the Torch travelled across two seas and seven war-ravaged countries, covering 3,160 kilometres in 12 days. With very few homes boasting television sets in 1948, the build-up and Relay was reported over the wireless, in newspapers and in pictorial commentaries in the Illustrated London News. As only the second modern Torch Relay in the history of the Games, the very notion of the Olympic Flame travelling to London was a novelty. Preparations caught the nation's imagination. In the ILN edition of 17 April, for example, a photograph recorded HMS Liverpool's departure from Portsmouth en route to the Mediterranean carrying 27 cases of Torches with an explanatory caption: 'One Torch will be lighted on Mount Olympus and the Flame passed on to other Torches which will be carried by marathon runners across Europe, the last Torch to be lit in the chain will be brought into the Stadium at the Olympic Ceremony.'

Under the heading, 'The Camera as Recorder of Items of General Interest', the ILN published photographs of the kindling of the Olympic Flame on 17 July. The process was overseen by a girl in full white dress – attended not by priestesses, but by a semicircle of bare-chested and barefoot men in dark baggy shorts, all suppliant on one knee. It turned out the ceremony was conducted by a Greek Girl Guide in a homemade robe, a stand-in for the girl originally chosen to travel from Athens to take the role. The civil war raging in Greece made it too dangerous to move about the country.

The plan had been to run 300 stages over 750km around Greece, but, after paying homage at the spot where the heart of Baron Pierre de Coubertin (the founder of the modern Olympic Movement) is buried, Corporal Dimitrelis of the Greek Army set off with the Torch along the road straight to the port of Katakolon. There the Flame was taken aboard a Greek destroyer which sailed for Corfu. It was then transferred to the British frigate Whitesand Bay, and the Royal Navy safeguarded its 22-hour crossing of the Adriatic. Arriving at Bari, the Torch was welcomed by Sandy Duncan, a British athletics coach, ready to be held aloft by relays of Italian soldiers running proudly in summer khakis. The party set off northwards, accompanied by military motorbikes and shadowed by an official Olympic Rolls-Royce carrying a reserve Flame in a lantern and spare Torches.

An Italian cadet in summer khaki uniform runs through the streets of Bari on 22 July 1948 undertaking one of the 1,416 legs run on the Relay of Peace. Bari was the first destination for the Torch outside of Greece, and it was proudly run through the streets by relays of Italian soldiers.

Crowds line the pavement on the bridge beneath the castle on 29 July 1948 as Gordon Wigley carries the Olympic Torch through Windsor and Eton on its way to Wembley. He was closely followed by the official Rolls-Royce containing a reserve Flame.

From Bari to London – via Foggia, Pescara, Ancona, Rimini, Bologna, Parma, Milan, the Simplon Pass, Lausanne, Geneva, Nantua, Besancon, Epinal, Nancy, Metz, Luxembourg City, Namur, Brussels, Tournai, Lille, Calais and Dover – the Relay only came to a halt twice. After running over the Simplon Pass into Switzerland, the cavalcade first paused in Lausanne to visit the actual grave of de Coubertin (whose last wish had been for his body to be laid to rest here and his heart buried separately in ancient Olympia). On the second stop, after crossing the bomb-scarred landscape of France, Luxembourg and Belgium, the Flame became the focus of an emotionally charged ceremony held at the Tomb of the Unknown Soldier in Brussels.

Photographic reportage could only offer glimpses of the Flame's journey across Europe, but its arrival on home soil was keenly anticipated by those who had received their letters of invitation to run a leg. The British runners were selected from clubs affiliated to the County Amateur Athletic Associations, one per club, with preference shown to the clubs on the route through Kent, Surrey, Berkshire and Buckinghamshire. 'It was terrific to receive that letter. My Dad was so proud of me,' recalls Charles McIlvenny who represented Stoke Poges Physical Recreation Club. Stages were mapped out at 5km intervals, with change-over points marked at places that provided shelter in case of bad weather. To be a chosen Torchbearer was not only an honour, but also a source of anxiety. Rumours that the Torch was incredibly heavy prompted one Torchbearer, a Kent butcher, to practise religiously for three weeks with a 4-pound (1.8kg) hammer to

Veteran runner H. J. Bignall (right) hands over the Olympic Flame to Fred Prevett at Redhill, Surrey, during the Flame's 22-hour journey from Dover to Wembley Stadium in 1948. Thousands lined the route to watch the symbol of peace make its way to the Opening Ceremony.

develop his arm muscles. Other runners confessed to sleepless nights, a common fear being that a downpour would quench the Flame on their leg.

On the evening of Wednesday 28 July, the Olympic Flame finally arrived in Calais where it was shepherded on board HMS *Bicester*. It reached Dover at 8.25pm, in the hands of Petty Officer Barnes. In recent years this southern corner of England had feared firepower from across the Channel. Now the country could welcome a friendly image of fire, a Flame of Peace. Today we are familiar with the Torch Relay as a format, but in 1948

the event must have seemed extraordinary. Out of pure curiosity, people of all ages – workers on annual breaks, schoolchildren on summer holidays, older people craving celebration after wartime privation – abandoned shops, offices and homes to throng streets and pavements as the Flame went by. It travelled through Dover, Canterbury, Charing, Maidstone, Redhill, Reigate, Dorking, Guildford, Ascot, Windsor, Slough and Uxbridge before arriving at Wembley's Empire Stadium on 29 July.

The extent to which less than 20 hours of Relay action on home soil captured the public imagination surprised everyone. The Flame passed spectators who stood shoulder to shoulder, craning necks, politely applauding the procession. People pushed relatives in wheelchairs and prams to witness the sight; others paused on their daily round, alighting from bikes, parking their hay trailer or car, even climbing up trees or lamp posts for a better view. There was something undeniably moving about the huge gatherings that took place throughout the night and at dawn. In Charing, Kent, at 1.30am, 3,000 people mobbed the Torchbearer. All available policemen were on crowd-control duties. Frank Verge, then 22, had been allotted the 4.03–4.17am slot between the Kent villages of Platt and Ightham: 'The road was lined with what seemed like hundreds of people. We had just gone through six years of war and I think the Olympic Games stood for more because it was a different kind of life – everyone was happy. It was a great thrill.'

Alan Wand, from Maidenhead, was 12 years old when the Flame came through his home town. 'All my friends and neighbours came out to watch the Torch arrive from Reading. There were about 150 of us gathered by the Pond House pub on the A4. We waited two hours for it to go past. We were good at waiting, having had to queue for everything during the war. When it eventually came it looked like a great big ice-cream cornet. We gave the man carrying it a jolly good cheer.'

Gordon Wigley carried the Torch across Windsor Town Bridge towards Eton. The Torch became so hot it was hard to hold and 'Wig' had to wrap his handkerchief around the handle to protect his hand from being burned. When Sid Binfield took over the Torch at the 'Burning Bush' lamp in Eton, Sid was so anxious that he ran off before anyone could take official handover photographs of the two Torchbearers.

Charles McIlvenny had roared back on his motorbike from holiday on Hayling Island, in Hampshire, arriving in time for his leg on the Slough to Uxbridge road. He was a keen athlete, known in his club for competing in the 440 yards. Even for a fit man, however, the 2-mile (3.2km) Torch run was not without its challenges. The Flame itself was only fuelled to burn for 15 minutes, so each runner had to keep up the pace to keep it alight within the designated time. No-one wanted the ignominy of a 'flame out' on their watch.

'I had to keep changing hands every two to three hundred yards because of the weight of it,' McIlvenny recalled of his run along a road lined with clamouring spectators. 'The two men who were with me kept shouting, "Give him room, let him breathe!" My mind was a bit of a blur. I was thinking,

"Goodness me, all these people here watching me." Some of them knew me and were shouting, "Good ole Mac, keep it up!" People were flocking around me, asking for autographs. Then it suddenly hits you that it is something you'll do once in a lifetime. You get that rush, thinking you're famous for a little while – I was just an ordinary athlete from an ordinary club carrying the Olympic Flame!' The bearers of the 1948 Relay were allowed to keep their Torches. An American offered McIlvenny a hundred pounds for his, but there was no way he was selling. He converted the Torch into a lamp, which has been proudly displayed in the family home for 64 years.

The penultimate bearer was R.S. Ellis of Wembley County Grammar School. Thankfully for posterity, the then 17-year-old described his experience in the school magazine: 'There were hundreds of people along the road and by the time the coach reached the Hop Bine in North Wembley, it was thousands. The crowd surged around, displaying such a keen interest in the Torch, which I tried to hide in my sweater, that I was afraid they would dismantle it there and then. However, a number of policemen, suitably big and broad, took the situation in hand and we instinctively made our way to the doorway of the Hop Bine. We looked around with a "What shall we do next?" air, for there was at least half an hour to wait. Then the landlord of the Hop Bine invited us in – this was succour indeed! We were offered a drink, and with much regret but some prudence I ordered a soda water. There were numerous interruptions by autograph hunters. In years to come the respective owners will wonder what the dickens R.S. Ellis is doing next to Winston Churchill [in their autograph books].'

Accompanied by numerous brass bands, the Flame finally arrived at the Empire Stadium at 4pm on Thursday 29 July. During the last two days of the Relay, spectators across northern Europe had basked in an idyllic holiday atmosphere. Temperatures reached a scorching 33.9°C and Torchbearers struggled in the heat. Wednesday 28 July proved the hottest day in London since 1911, part of a mini-heatwave in which Paris experienced its highest-ever recorded temperature of 40.4°C. After completing his leg, Charles McIllvenny took the Torch into a hospital where his father was being treated. 'The Torch was passed around the ward for everyone to hold,' he remarked. 'They all felt better.'

As has since become the custom, there had been considerable speculation as to who would have the honour of running the last leg into the arena to light the Olympic Cauldron. In 1948 the bookies' favourites included Sydney Wooderson, an outstanding middle-distance runner, and HRH the Duke of Edinburgh who had married Princess Elizabeth in the previous year. But, in keeping with their concept of reaffirming Olympic values, the organisers wanted the Relay of Peace to culminate with someone whose physical looks radiated Youth and Vitality. Poor old Wooderson, bespectacled and only 1.68 metres tall, did not fit the bill. Instead the role went to John Mark, a 22-year-old medical student, who had been president of the Cambridge University Athletics Club in 1947 and had also represented Great Britain at the 400m. Fitness issues prevented Mark's inclusion in Olympic track

action, but after his clandestine selection for that final leg he began training in secret for the most iconic athletic role of all. Carrying the Olympic Torch on the last lap with the arm extended took enormous strength. 'A white Rolls began to turn up at St Mary's [hospital] to take him to the Stadium and back,' one contemporary recalled, in the *Cranleighan* magazine for fellow alumni of Mark's school. 'He wouldn't tell anyone what was going on, but when it happened, and the other students found out, they were livid. When they saw him they used to light their cigarette lighter and run round him in a circle. When they said he looked like a Greek god, it was right. He did.'

Wembley was packed for the Opening Ceremony. Six thousand competing athletes from 58 nations entered the Stadium. Speeches were delivered, 7,000 pigeons released and, off-stage, a 21-gun salute sounded. At precisely 4.30pm – before a Royal Party that included King George VI, Queen Elizabeth, Prime Minister Clement Attlee, Queen Mary, the Duke and Duchess of Gloucester and the Duchess of Kent, and a dense crowd of 80,000 spectators – came what *The Times* described as the most dramatic event of all: the arrival of the Olympic Flame. As Mark entered Wembley, a roar erupted. No sooner had he started his lap of the Stadium than many of the athletes who had gathered in the middle of the track broke ranks and spilt over on to the cinder running track, willing the Flame on its way. The *Guardian* report of the event had echoes of a military despatch: 'The Flame was white against the golden light of the late afternoon and it burned with the resolution of an incendiary bomb. [Mark] began to make his way round, leaving a trail of white heat on the shale surface, running with a perfection of style not easily attained when one arm must be still.'

The small flicker that had burst into life in the Peloponnese had arrived in Wembley – a symbolic moment that every observer was keen to describe in their own words. As the Rt Hon Philip Noel-Baker, the government minister responsible for the Games, wrote in the preface to the 1948 Official Report: 'No one who saw it will forget that thrilling spectacle. Tall and handsome like a young Greek god, [Mark] stood for a moment in the sunshine, then ran in perfect rhythm round the track, saluted again and lit the Flame in the bowl where, day and night, it burned until the Games were done.'

Fanny Blankers-Koen, who went on to win four gold medals at the Games, said: 'When the athlete carrying the Torch entered the Stadium every woman swooned. He was a magnificent specimen of manhood. I tried to arrange a rendezvous with him after I had won my four gold medals, but I was told he was too shy to meet me. What a pity!' According to the *Cranleighan* report, not everyone was swept up in the moment. As Mark appeared it was claimed the Queen [subsequently the Queen Mother] was overheard saying: 'Dear me, what a pity they did not get that dear little Sydney [Wooderson] to do it.'

As a tonic to the nation, the reverence accorded the arrival of the Olympic Flame was beautifully summed up by Roger Bannister and Harold Abrahams. 'I had the feeling that we were witnessing sacred rites being performed in an open-air cathedral,' said

A roar erupts as British athlete John Mark bears the Olympic Torch on a lap of Wembley Stadium at the Opening Ceremony of the 1948 Games. 'Every woman swooned,' said Fanny Blankers-Koen, who went on to win four gold medals.

Bannister, while Abrahams reflected: 'After long years of almost unending national and international strain and stress, here was the light of a flame which crossed a continent without hindrance, caused frontiers to disappear, gathered unprecedented crowds, and lit the path to a brighter future for the youth of the world.'

More than 60 years later, difficult economic conditions were again in evidence. This time, however, the Torch Relay was less about solace and more about celebration – of the Games, the Relay and all those who helped to bring them about. From the sacred Flame's arrival on home soil on 19 May to its transfer to the Cauldron at the culmination of the Opening Ceremony on 27 July, the Torch Relay brought the Olympic Games to within 16km of 95 per cent of the UK population. It was an epic, joyful journey whose spirit was captured in the 2012 theme of a 'Moment to Shine'.

The itinerary for VIP passenger 'Symbolic Flame', travelling from Greece to the Olympic Stadium in London, ran as follows:

10–17 May Lit in Olympia in the traditional hour-long ceremony, and carried around the Greek mainland and islands.

18 May Disembarked at Royal Naval Air Station Culdrose, near Helston in Cornwall, on board a gold-liveried British Airways flight BA2012. The Flame had its own seat on the plane, receiving special authorisation from the Civil Aviation Authority to travel in a secured ceremonial lantern.

19 May The Torch Relay set off from Land's End on a 70-day odyssey including 66 evening celebrations, six island visits and one day outside the United Kingdom (Dublin on 6 June). Some 8,000 Torchbearers carried the Flame 300m each.

To take the Flame to within 16km, or an hour's journey, of the vast majority of people in the United Kingdom was an enormous task – a great claim to have been able to fulfil, and the result of two years' planning and consultation. After winning the bid to host the Games in 2005, the London Organising Committee of the Olympic and Paralympic Games (LOCOG) established the Nations and Regions Group (NRG) to engage the breadth of the United Kingdom, both in determining the Torch Relay route and in selecting the inspirational Torchbearers. Composed of 12 senior representatives from business and sport – nine from the English regions and one each from Scotland, Wales and Northern Ireland – the NRG rallied local authorities and community groups such as the National Trust, Scout Association and Blue Light services to throw ideas into the pot and submit them to LOCOG. The trickiest challenge of route setting was trying to please everybody, but the NRG usefully doubled up as a diplomatic service at grass roots.

Stephen Doran was the Senior Operations Manager, travelling in the command car directly behind the Torchbearers for every one of those 70 days. He explained the intricate mapping-out process that shaped the Relay route. 'The starting point is always scope and budget. Then it's big-picture considerations. What major events did we need to avoid, such as the British Grand Prix at Silverstone, because accommodation and resources would be taken up? What events did we want to tie into? Where would we be during big UEFA Euro 2012 fixtures? Lands End, we knew, was the starting point. On Friday and Saturday nights we wanted to be in cities with large population centres with sufficient infrastructure to support our celebration-site crowds of 10,000 plus. We looked at our remote locations – the Orkneys, Shetlands, Western Isles, Isle of Man, Guernsey and Jersey – and tried to fit that into the plan considering local sensitivities. Sunday remains a very religious day in the Western Isles, so although we arrived there on a Sunday, we would not do anything until Monday.

'Then we considered logistics. How far could we go in a day? How many Torchbearers did we need to use in a day: 8,000 bearers in 70 days, an average of 110 per day, running at an average of 4mph, so we allocated an average of seven hours a day for running, which would take up 48 miles. So we knew we had to drive between locations. It worked out, on average, that we drove 60–70 miles a day and the rest was running. That means 75 per cent of each day was spent running and 25 per cent driving. We had to overlay overnight accommodation (for 150 core crew members, but up to 450 people altogether) and that was based on invitation, dependent totally on whether local authorities wanted to host us.'

In the course of marking the route on a vast map on his office table – highlighting potential routes and counting the communities that could be included from 7am to 7pm – Doran also had to factor in the planned diversions. Other Host Nations have transported the Flame in outlandish ways: via satellite (Montreal 1976); on board a supersonic plane (Albertville 1992); by parachute (Lillehammer 1994); underwater (at the Great Barrier Reef for

Outlandish modes of transport: the Olympic Flame has travelled via satellite, by supersonic plane, by parachute and on a camel. Here it is taken underwater at the Great Barrier Reef prior to the Sydney Games of 2000.

Sydney 2000); by showcasing it in canoes, steamboats, on camels and so on. Torch Relay organisers look to embrace the Olympic motto 'Faster, Higher, Stronger' as well as athletes. The focus for a modern Relay had to be much more than on a single runner pounding down a road. 'So we mixed it up with interesting modes of transport pertinent to certain areas,' said Doran, and they proved a resounding success. The Flame was transported on two wheels by a TT motorcycle sidecar on the Isle of Man, by a cob horse in Aberaeron, by zip wire from the top of the Tyne Bridge to the Gateshead riverside, in a punt along the River Cam, courtesy of a powerboat in Bristol Harbour and via the narrow gauge Ffestiniog Railway, among others. All these scenarios, and many others, presented idiosyncratic security and operational challenges.

Doran's advance team drove the route three times to test it was logistically feasible and to match up all the Torchbearer modes to the right individual bearers. The team also tested the alternative methods of transport for the Flame and ensured that scheduled photo opportunities and Torchbearer splits (occasions when the convoy stopped for the Torchbearer to run down a pedestrianised area, for example) worked within the prescribed timings. The result was the Day Book, in which notes for daily schedules stretched to 150–200 pages per day. A fourth and final route drive fixed the positioning of the 8,000 Torchbearers along the route, identifying every single exchange point. Every Torchbearer received a letter in April 2012, indicating exactly where they would start and finish.

The detailed logistics of the convoy – that is, vehicles, drivers, ferry and flight bookings, equipment and distribution of everything from Torches to snacks and sun cream – were the responsibility of Mark Richards, Logistics Manager, Olympic Torch Relays at London 2012. The convoy comprised nearly 50 crew vehicles: 15 saloon vehicles, three Mini Countrymen, seven estate cars, two minibuses, two MPVs, 10 shuttle buses for Torchbearers, a coach for the Metropolitan Police's mobile command post, a horse box for the media, a coach for the three Presenting Partners (Coca Cola, Lloyds TSB and Samsung), three 18,000kg trucks to carry equipment (from ratchet straps to Torches to spare police motorbikes) and another truck for 250 items of overnight baggage. All vehicles required regular refuelling and washing, as well as secure overnight parking.

'The Presenting Partners each had between 20 and 25 vehicles as well, so the whole travelling circus was around 140 or 150 vehicles. On television, the public only saw 14 or 15. The rest were working in advance, in the rear, or satellite-ing around to sustain the operation,' explained Richards. 'We worked on a three-day loop around a network of UPS depots to collect new batches of Torches and gas canisters and drop off the used ones. Some of the cars were fitted out like the cockpits of fighter jets. We had rallying computers, which measure to the metre, a computer system linked to Steve Doran's in the command car and variable message display light boards on the roofs. It was a rolling business of incredible accuracy. Torchbearers were dropped and collected within precise parameters of speed and distance, mapped out to the numbers on telegraph poles or lamp posts. Before I took this job, I didn't even know that telegraph poles had numbers on them.'

Richards' car racked up more mileage than any other vehicle. His tasks included satellite-ing around the Relay in his estate car, preparing for the arrival of the convoy in the evening, issuing snacks, drinks and sun cream to flagging crew members and helping to offload overnight luggage bags. 'That involved shifting 250 big bags into hotel lobbies and up to bedrooms for 70 consecutive nights,' he said. 'It meant all hands on deck and a few blisters.'

Before the Torch Relay set off, Simon Williams (chief enabler of a good night's sleep, daily sustenance and clean laundry for the Relay crew) declared he would only have done a good job if no one knew he and his team existed. Working in pairs, and leap-frogging overnight destinations, his team prepared each stopover venue with signage, trolleys, ramps, spare refreshments and tape to cordon off car parks. They never saw the actual Flame, but considered it a privilege to ensure crew welfare. 'It was a 70-day operation of incredible intensity. No travelling circus or touring event moves with this mass of people, with this frequency. We had lots of youngsters working very long hours, potentially exhausted and missing home comforts. The earliest start was 5.19am, which meant breakfast at 4.19am. Our role was to maintain morale, motivate, give treats, read minds and faces, know when to give a high five or simply say "Here's your key, go and get a good night's sleep".'

Long before the convoy hit the road in May 2012, Williams worked in tandem with the route-setters to fix accommodation. The challenges were enormous. 'I was booking for 300 to 450 people, asking hoteliers for one-night-only bookings, within the constraints of a tight budget. Not many of our overnight stopover points had a big conference hotel. We needed rooms with twin beds, and hotels usually only have a maximum designation of 30 per cent twin rooms. So then it was a case of finding secondary hotels no further than a 10-minute walk away. Every night we also needed banqueting space and a kitchen that could cater a rolling buffet for 300 in two shifts of 150. We needed 100 square metres of accessible space near the foyer to set up the convoy office with noticeboards for start times, rotas, and so on. We also needed mega parking space.

'I had to make enquiries keeping secret the nature of our "large touring group", because it might give away the route before it had been officially announced. We had to beg. "We are prestigious," I said, "although we are working to a very tight budget. And when we come to your hotel, you will feel the buzz, the love: the whole town will be alive and we will bring that

into your hotel!" In the end, we had just seven nights when we were all under one roof. In Aberystwyth we were spread across eight different hotels. In Northumberland, on one night, we were divided between three different towns. We stayed in caravan parks, student halls of residence, even a golfing spa hotel. No stone was left unturned.'

Lunchtime food was provided in school ground sites by caterers, well briefed on the nutritional needs of everyone from sedentary car crew to the police runners who ran the equivalent of half a marathon a day. Evening sustenance came in the form of a rolling 14-day menu – lasagne only once a fortnight! – and regular fun-themed culinary nights. Williams challenged chefs to go crazy and make their hotel and home town memorable. Once a week, the cuisine of previous Olympic Host Nations was celebrated with the likes of Spanish, Greek and Chinese menus.

What to do with 450 people's dirty underwear? The convoy team were kept clean and fragrant thanks to an arrangement with an industrial launderer that collected and returned clothes on a three-day cycle. Each team member had a unique bar code ironed into T-shirts, jeans and so on. Smalls went into individually coded mesh bags. 'On arrival in Bristol, for example, all the clean laundry was delivered with the overnight baggage,' Williams explained. 'Distributing luggage to hotel rooms took four hours a day anyway, but on clean laundry days we'd also have to marry up laundry bags to luggage so that it was all ready for the crew in their bedrooms. We also had a left laundry rail in our office and several rules: No Angora knits! No sequins!'

Torch Designs: Berlin 1936 to London 2012

Summer 1936 Berlin

Summer 1948 London

Winter 1952 Oslo

Summer 1952 Helsinki

Winter 1956 Cortina d'Ampezzo

Summer 1956 Melbourne

Winter 1960 Squaw Valley

Summer 1960 Rome

Winter 1964 Innsbruck

Summer 1964 Tokyo

Winter 1968 Grenoble

Summer 1968 Mexico

Winter 1972 Sapporo

Summer 1972 Munich

Winter 1976 Innsbruck

Summer 1976 Montreal

THE FULL LINE-UP: Olympic Torches, featured in Summer and Winter Games from 1936 onwards, show remarkable variation in design and construction. However, Torches must always contain the same three elements: fuel (to support the Flame), a fuel delivery system (so that the Flame shines from the top of the Torch) and a lightweight, aerodynamic structure.

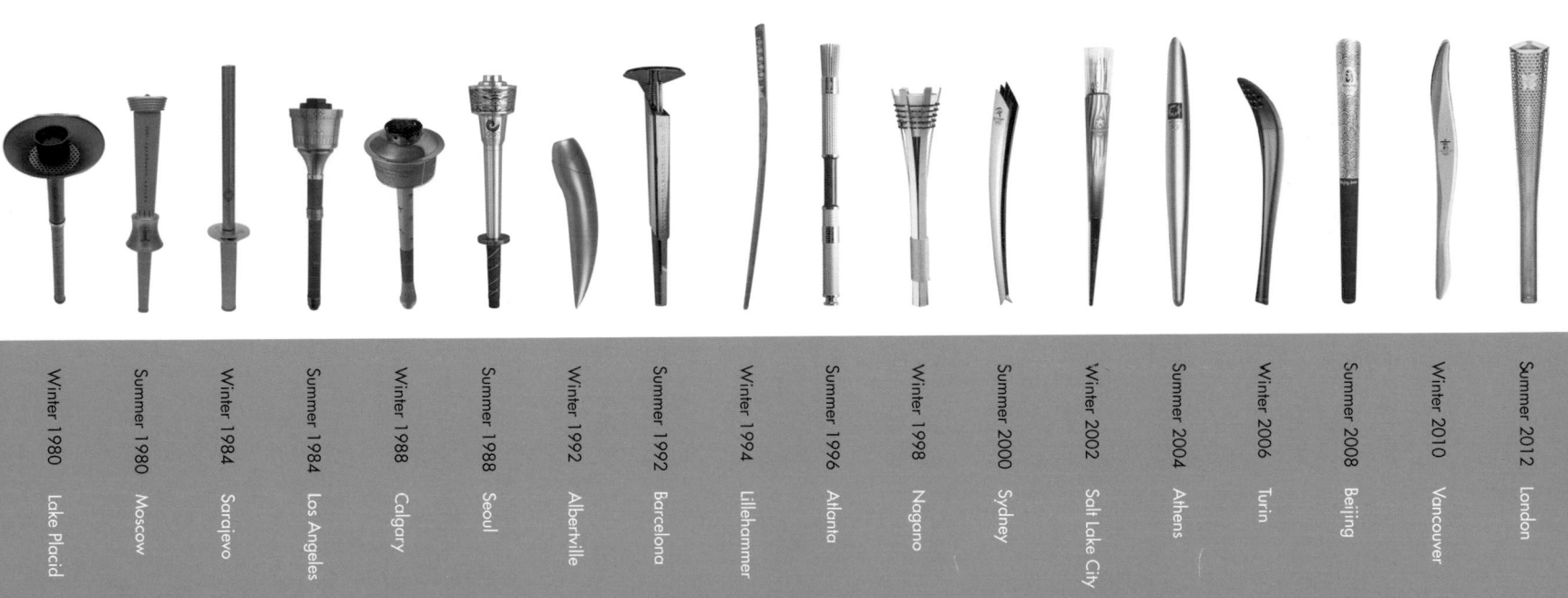

Winter 1980 — Lake Placid

Summer 1980 — Moscow

Winter 1984 — Sarajevo

Summer 1984 — Los Angeles

Winter 1988 — Calgary

Summer 1988 — Seoul

Winter 1992 — Albertville

Summer 1992 — Barcelona

Winter 1994 — Lillehammer

Summer 1996 — Atlanta

Winter 1998 — Nagano

Summer 2000 — Sydney

Winter 2002 — Salt Lake City

Summer 2004 — Athens

Winter 2006 — Turin

Summer 2008 — Beijing

Winter 2010 — Vancouver

Summer 2012 — London

Celebrity runners, from actors and Olympians to sports stars, lent their lustre to the Torch Relay – not just by their superstar presence, but also in their often touching or impassioned ties to the geographical stretch they were allotted to run. The real emotional dynamic, however, stemmed from the initial selection process of the 7,200 'ordinary but extraordinary' Torchbearers who carried the Olympic message around the country and enjoyed their 'moment to shine'. Each Torchbearer had to be nominated as an inspiring person by someone else, and selection was a tribute to individuals hailed as uplifting in personality or notable in their contribution to society. The LOCOG nominations process took place from May to June 2011, with Relay Presenting Partners Coca-Cola, Lloyds TSB and Samsung also holding their own nomination campaigns. Selection panels, consisting of leaders of councils, scout groups, policemen and firemen, were formed in each of the 12 Nations and Regions. Two people from each panel read every nomination, and a potential bearer had to impress both to be considered as a Torchbearer.

The standard of inspiring nomination statements was remarkable. Many of the Torchbearers were aged between 12 and 24; their life stories pricked tears and stirred emotions. Uniform in their appearance (a regulation white top with stand-up collar and cricket-style trousers), they proved to be incredibly diverse in terms of background, age and achievement. Along the 300m they ran in the glow of the Olympic Flame we learned snippets of people's heroic deeds, courage and commitment. The Torchbearers included Coastguard volunteers, foster carers, charity fund-raisers, youth workers, prison welfare campaigners, life-changing teachers and devoted family members caring for a child, parent or partner. There were those who had overcome disabilities, illness and personal tragedy to help others; lion-hearted personalities who had resolved to improve conditions for children in Africa or who stood out as role models in their communities. Who didn't smile, laugh, shed a tear, rejoice in individual achievement and feel a tingle down the spine?

Edward Barber and Jay Osgerby won the opportunity to design the Torch through a competitive tender run by LOCOG and the Design Council. 'When we were shortlisted, we received a briefing document, literally a book: 80 pages of information on everything from history to performance criteria. For instance, the Torch had to operate across a certain temperature range (-10 to 40+°C), in winds gusting up to 75mph, at an altitude of 6,000 feet above sea level with a constant flame height and luminosity. We would normally give three months to a project of that complexity and scale, involving production and technical know-how, but we had 10 days. It wasn't an issue. We worked through the night. From the moment we watched the announcement of London's winning bid, we were absolutely determined to win,' said Osgerby, perhaps inspired by a sense of family continuum. His great uncle had cycled around London on the day the Torch arrived in 1948 and watched it go into the Empire Stadium.

Their winning design was an Olympic Torch 'for our time'. The golden, three-sided form was perforated by 8,000 circles, representing the stories of the 8,000 Torchbearers who ran 8,000 miles. The triangular form arose from the trinities that recurred in the brief. There were the three Olympic Movement values of respect, excellence and friendship; the three elements of the Olympic motto 'Faster, Higher, Stronger'; the fact that this was the third occasion, after 1908 and 1948, that London had hosted the Games; and the legacy aims of London 2012 in terms of Business, Sport and Education. 'We realised early on that it needed to have a narrative in the design, a story to give meaning,' Barber revealed. 'It was important to us that it felt like a piece of sporting equipment, not a trophy. We were keen to make one of the lightest Torches, but also one high enough to be seen over a crowd as many of the Torchbearers were young people. We wanted to design a Torch that was both contemporary looking and cutting-edge in manufacturing techniques.'

True to Barber and Osgerby's intention, the manufacturing process was indeed cutting-edge. The design duo worked closely with Basildon-based product engineers Tecosim and Coventry manufacturers Premier Sheet Metal to develop the prototypes for the Torch before it went into mass production. Made from aluminium alloy 5182 – strong, light, available in the right thickness and affordable – the Torch consisted of four component parts: a top cap, a bottom cap and two skins. Across its length (799.5mm) the skins never touch and the holes are slightly offset.

The holes were a challenge to create, and the solution was provided by the world's fastest 2-D laser machine, installed in a factory in Coventry. Cutting four holes per second, it made the equivalent of 96 Torch skins per day in the form of flat sheets of aluminium, representing the inner and outer layer. Each sheet went through three different presses to create the triangular form by folding the inner and outer skins. These went back into a 3-D laser machine, which welded the seam in four seconds, and then cut holes back in over the top of that weld seam, so that the seam itself was invisible. The outer skin was then cleaned up while the inner skin underwent some tinkering for functionality (to attach to wheelchairs, bicycles, rowing boats). The two skins were then fitted together by welding on the end caps.

'The clever bit was the polishing, which hides all the weld seams,' explained Mark Scholey, Programme Manager for the Relay. 'Each Torch was plated – given its dress finish – and went off to another supplier to undergo a process called physical vapour deposition (PVD). This was unbelievable science, involving a ball of plasma bouncing around inside a chamber. The chamber held 10 Torches at a time. After two hours, they emerged gold.' No previous Torch has been so gloriously gold – fitting for a symbol of light that would reveal the Host Nation's varied landscape. 'It would have been really easy for us to do a steel finish and we have a tendency as a nation to be reticent, but this is a great chance to show off and celebrate,' Osgerby observed.

The circles helped to ensure that heat was quickly dissipated, without being conducted down the handle, while the perforated texture provided extra grip. The holes also offered a unique level of transparency, allowing bearers to look into the heart of the

ABOVE LEFT MIDDLE AND RIGHT: At The Premier Group in Coventry, each Torch skin went through three different presses to create its triangular form, designed to reflect the three words of the Olympic motto – faster, higher, stronger, the three Olympic Movement values, and the third time London has hosted the Games. The 8,000 symbolic holes in each Torch were cut by the world's fastest 2-D laser machine.

IMAGE BELOW AND RIGHT: Produced from aluminium alloy 5182 - strong, light, available in the right thickness and affordable – each Torch is made up of four component parts: a top cap, a bottom cap and two skins. No previous Torch has been so gloriously gold: 'We have a tendency as a nation to be reticent, but this is the chance to show off and celebrate,' said designer Jay Osgerby.

Torch and view the burner system that kept the Olympic Flame alive. 'One of the interesting human aspects of the project was the balance of design and functionality,' said Scholey. 'The design, by common consent, was very pretty, but the holes also meant that the Flame was exposed from every angle. We think Bullfinch [the Birmingham-based LPG Gas specialists and manufacturers] designed the most robust burner system that has ever gone into an Olympic Torch – basically because they had to.'

In the past Torches have come in all shapes and sizes: slim and fluted, robustly classic, ultra-skinny, even slug-shaped. They have resembled reeds bound by twine, a plate atop a handle, an icicle. Some have been fastidiously referenced, such as Sydney's Torch, which boasted echoes of the silhouette of the Opera House and a boomerang, accented with Pacific blue; others have been robustly architectural, such as the mini Calgary Tower that honoured the Calgary 1988 Winter Games. Sometimes they have generated the wrong kind of story. The Relay route prior to the Mexico City 1968 Games followed that taken by Christopher Columbus from Europe to the New World. However, the bold adventure was punctuated by minor explosions and mildly scorched athletes when the solid fuel mixture proved unexpectedly volatile. Special pressurised Torches had to be used prior to the Munich 1972 Games when temperatures hit 46°C en route from Greece to Germany. In the international Relay organised for the Beijing 2008 Games, Steve Redgrave ran out of Wembley Stadium with a Torch leaking fuel down the inside, threatening to burn his hands. Anecdotal horror stories from previous Games

include Torchbearers who became carried away, jumped in the air, fell over and landed on their Torch; or the person who greeted the next Torchbearer with a hug, Torch still in hand, and set them on fire from behind.

Before it went into mass production, the London 2012 Olympic Torch went through simulation tests, drop tests, stress tests, strength tests, upside down tests. 'We dropped the Torch from three metres on its base and on its top – the two worst-case scenarios – and not only did it stay intact, but alight,' reported Scholey. 'We were determined to beat the record of least "flame outs", which meant suffering fewer than the seven experienced at the Turin 2006 Games. We even went as far as seeking clarity on the definition of a flame out!'

To make sure the Flame could withstand all weather conditions the Torch was tested in BMW's climatic testing facility in Munich. 'Wind tunnels are very good for simulating consistent 50mph winds and solid rain, but we needed gusting winds, rain squalls, drizzle and everything else this country might have thrown at us,' said Scholey. 'We took it up Snowdon to test it at altitude. I took Olympic athlete Donna Fraser to Dungeness and had her running up and down the beach, with one of our engineers pretending to be Luke Skywalker waving the Torch around. Before the Relay started, I could assure you that you can burn the Torch upside down and it was perfectly safe.'

The London 2012 Paralympic Torch shares the same core Barber and Osgerby design as the Olympic Torch, but with a mirror finish. The Paralympic Relay, taking place between 25 and 29 August, will run from Stoke Mandeville to the Olympic Stadium, celebrating Britain's heritage as the birthplace of Paralympic sport. The first Flame-lighting event of the Relay will take place in London after the Closing Ceremony of the Olympic Games. Flames will also be lit in Greater Belfast, Edinburgh and Cardiff, with each city showcasing an idiosyncratic style in their Flame-lighting method, hosting an evening Flame Festival and a tour of local community groups. Each Flame will then travel to Stoke Mandeville where they will be ceremonially combined at a Paralympic Flame Lighting Ceremony on 28 August to create the London 2012 Paralympic Flame – a symbol to inspire disabled people throughout the world to transform their lives through sport.

Torchbearers have been nominated for the Paralympic values of energy and endeavour that they display so admirably in everyday life. Each Torchbearer has an inspirational story of courage, determination and the desire for equality, striving to push the boundaries of what is achievable. Working in teams of five, the Torchbearers will carry the Flame on its final 24-hour journey to the Olympic Stadium to light the Cauldron at the Paralympic Games Opening Ceremony. The dazzling mirror-finish of the Torch will illuminate the special atmosphere during the dark hours of the overnight Relay.

The first Paralympic Torch Relay took place at the Seoul 1988 Games, where there were 282 Torchbearers, 111 of whom were disabled people. Since then Organising Committees of the Games have strived to make sure the Paralympic Torch Relay touches as many lives as possible. At Athens 2004, the Flame was lit at the Hephaestus Temple in Athens – a particularly apt location as Hephaestus, the Greek god of fire and manufacturing, had a disability. Once lit, some 680 Torchbearers carried the Flame through 54 municipalities, heralding the coming of the Games. Four years later, at the Beijing 2008 Games, the Flame was lit at the Temple of Heaven in Beijing, before being carried by 850 Torchbearers on a route around the country that was intended to capture the characters of ancient and modern China.

On its progress around the United Kingdom, the Olympic Torch revealed a compelling mix of past and present to those watching highlights on television or via the BBC online service. Castles and cathedrals, bridges and stately homes mingled with modern cityscapes and bustling markets, innovative contemporary buildings and intriguing artworks. It also revealed landscapes of natural beauty, from rivers to mountains, rolling farmland to coasts and moors. All corners of the nation joined the celebrations: the drama of St Michael's Mount in Cornwall, the elegance of the Royal Crescent in Bath, the mysterious standing stones of Stonehenge and the World Heritage Site of Durdle Door on Dorset's Jurassic Coast. A powerful, diverse backdrop was conjured by locations such as Caerphilly Castle, Mount Snowdon, Shropshire's Iron Bridge and Antony Gormley's *Another Place* on Crosby Beach in Sefton. In following the Flame's journey everyone could 'visit' legendary landmarks such as the Giant's Causeway in Northern Ireland, the Forth Rail Bridge in Edinburgh, Hadrian's Wall – and the Olympic Park itself.

The itinerary of the Relay brought to life so many parts of the United Kingdom and reminded us of their diverse local flavours. The fun now is in reminiscing about how the Flame touched more than 1,000 villages, towns and cities along its journey – and how, in particular, our home towns earned their place in history. The strong response to LOCOG's Line the Streets initiative meant no decorative thought was wasted: the call to plant golden marigolds along the route, for example, was a nice nod to our domestic gardening heritage. From start to finish, communities pushed boundaries in their efforts to shine. They embraced the gold party theme whole-heartedly and lined the route en masse with imaginative gleaming outfits, fancy dress, gilded faces, flame-themed paraphernalia and gold-and-white bunting. After all the planning and anticipation, the Olympic Torch Relay brought the Games to the nation in a festival of colour, anticipation and delight. And when the Flame finally entered the Stadium to take its place in the Olympic Cauldron, the world was primed for epic sporting action – at last, the Games could begin.

At 7.24pm on Friday 18 May BA2012 'The Firefly', a gold-liveried A319, landed at the Royal Naval Air Station Culdrose in Cornwall. Minutes later a tiny spark inside a golden ceremonial lantern was carried down the aircraft steps by the Princess Royal. Hundreds of people waved gold and white flags to greet the Olympic Flame.

Chapter 1
19 to 25 May

Highlights

On Saturday 19 May people began to gather before dawn at Land's End to watch the start of the London 2012 Olympic Torch Relay. Anticipation mounted in the early morning light as the waiting crowds strained to catch the sound of the search and rescue helicopter bringing the Flame from RNAS Culdrose where it had stayed overnight. Ben Ainslie, three times Olympic champion sailor, member of The Royal Cornwall Yacht Club in Falmouth and now Torchbearer 001, hovered under the iconic First and Last signpost with the eyes of the world upon him. 'It was a pretty surreal feeling waiting for the helicopter to fly around the headland with the Flame. It was a beautiful morning, very calm, the sun rising, but it was one of the more nervous moments of my life,' he recalled.

At 7am the Sea King helicopter, which had flown many missions as part of 771 Naval Air Squadron, came into view, revealing a specially painted gold rotor blade. It landed safely and Lieutenant Commander Richard Full, a member of the Royal Navy Search and Rescue squadron, carried the Lantern containing the Olympic Flame carefully towards the famous signpost. Ben Ainslie's Torch was lit and he carried it over to the crowd, who pressed forward in their excitement. 'I was blown away by the reaction,' the Olympian revealed.

And then the Relay began – the start of a 70-day, 8,000-mile journey that would take the spirit of the Games to more than 1,000 towns, villages and cities around the country. Week 1 showcased a passionate community spirit along a route from the most southwesterly point of Cornwall to Cardiff. By late afternoon on Day 1 the Torch reached the Eden Project, to be greeted by families with homemade 'Torches'. They had come to witness the adventurer Ben Fogle ascend with the Flame in a helium balloon within the Rainforest Biome. The balloon, used by scientists to tend the treetop canopy, rose 50m into the humid heights with Fogle brandishing the Lantern from a swing seat. 'That was one of the most amazing experiences … it was extraordinary looking out on a sea of people and all the plants below,' he enthused on his return to *terra firma*.

Over the next six days the gloriously sunny Relay passed through many famous and historic sites: Torre Abbey, Dunster Castle, Wells Cathedral, Glastonbury Tor, Clifton Suspension Bridge (where fireworks saluted the Flame's progress along Isambard Kingdom Brunel's structure), Cheltenham Racecourse, Gloucester Cathedral

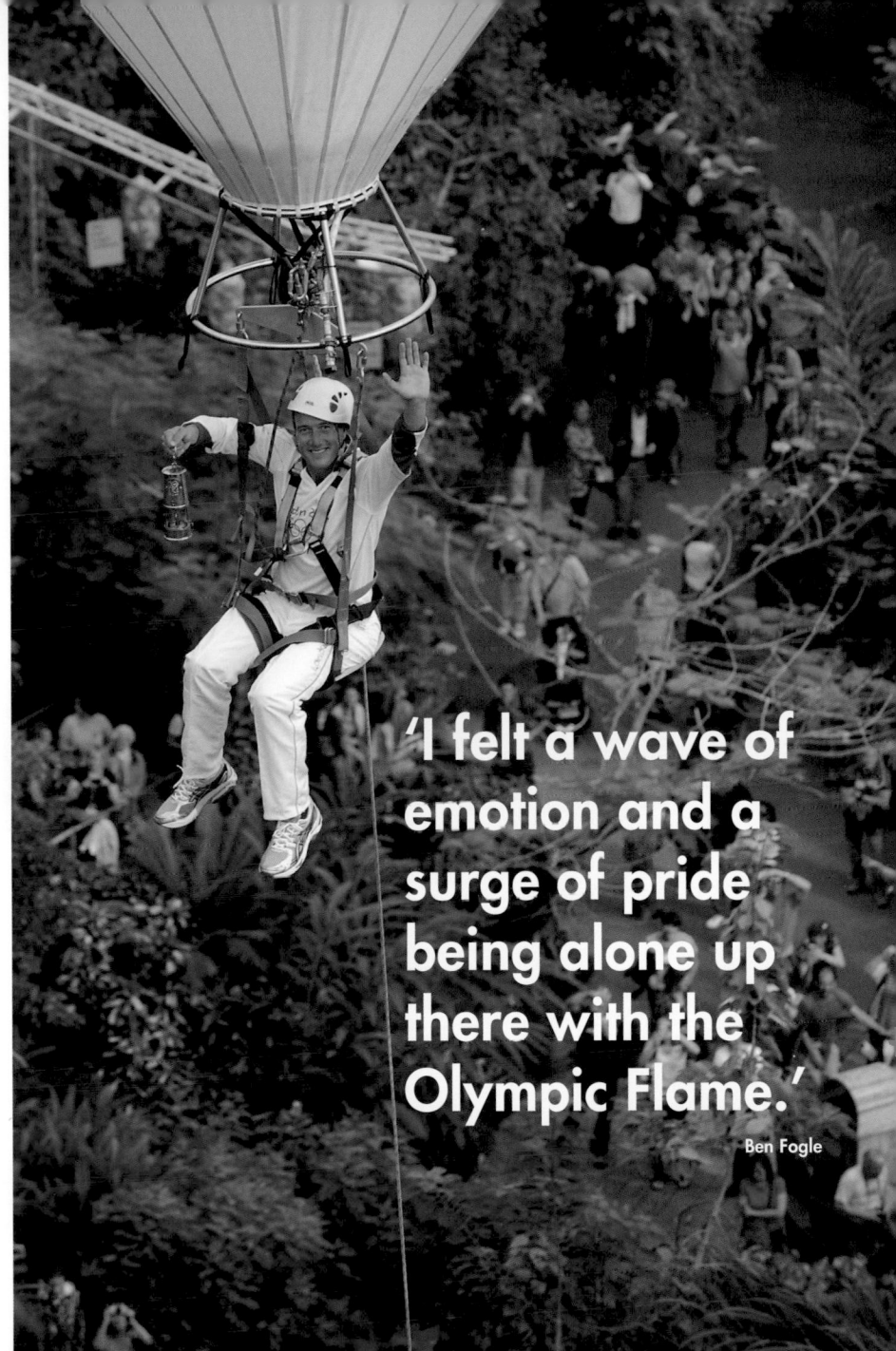

Adventurer Ben Fogle takes the Olympic Flame in a Lantern up to the humid heights of the Rainforest Biome in the Eden Project, Cornwall.

and Cardiff Castle (which added an Olympic moment to its 2000-year story as Roman garrison, Norman stronghold and fairytale fantasy in Victorian gothic). The Flame was held aloft in an electric-powered community boat, survived a powerboat ride, trotted on horseback, and chuffed along on the footplate of a Severn Valley steam train. At the West Midlands Safari Park two African elephants gave the Flame a 'trunk salute', waving a Union flag for five minutes. Their display mirrored the hundreds of thousands of people who lined the streets of their towns and villages, bursting into camera-clicking fervour as the Flame approached.

Against a colourful backdrop of flags, brass bands, balloons, bunting, Morris Men, face-paint, wedding parties, overhead helicopters and the odd police outrider high-fiving schoolchildren, the Torchbearers formed a proud human chain. Celebrity participants ranged from Olympians Jonathan Edwards, Sharron Davies, David Hemery, Amy Williams, Lynn Davies and Jane Holderness-Roddam to potential London 2012 stars Jason Gardener and Darren Campbell. Former England cricketer and Somerset captain Marcus Trescothick carried the Torch in Taunton, and Wales rugby captain Sam Warburton also took a turn, as did the rock band Muse and rapper Will.i.am. Yet this was mostly the opportunity of 'extraordinary ordinary people' – unsung heroes who worked selflessly for good causes or who had overcome illness – to relish their moment to shine, and this they did in magnificent style.

'I felt a wave of emotion and a surge of pride being alone up there with the Olympic Flame.'

Ben Fogle

OPPOSITE: Ben Ainslie, three-time Olympic gold medallist, waves to the Sea King helicopter delivering the Olympic Flame to Land's End, the starting point of the Torch Relay. Crowds gathered around the iconic signpost in the early morning sunshine, and the specially painted rotor blade gleamed gold.

ABOVE LEFT: Torchbearers Sarah Blight and Wendy Pittendrigh exchange the Olympic Flame with a traditional Torch 'kiss' on the beach at Marazion, Cornwall, close to the famous landmark of St Michael's Mount.

BELOW LEFT: Land's End at dawn. Crowds revel in a day of emotion as the Olympic Flame embarks on its symbolic 70-day journey.

'Look at that kids, right in front of you, that's history.'

Colin Thomas from Redruth, Cornwall, to his four children, Jackson 11, Taylor 10, Grace 6 and Phoebe 3 at Land's End

'To be the first normal person – I mean not an athlete – to run is amazing. It's a weird feeling. It makes me feel patriotic: proud to be where I'm from...'

Tassy Swallow, 18, from St Ives, who campaigns for surfing to be recognised as an Olympic sport

ABOVE: The veteran commentator Barry Davies, 74, is 'really delighted' to carry the Torch in Plymouth on the first day of the Relay. London 2012 will be his 19th Olympic Games, an event he relishes as much as ever.

RIGHT: The Torch Security Team transfer the Olympic Flame into a Lantern for safekeeping. Certain forms of transport, from Flight BA2012 The Firefly to trains or Fogle's helium-filled balloon, require a more secure container for the precious Flame.

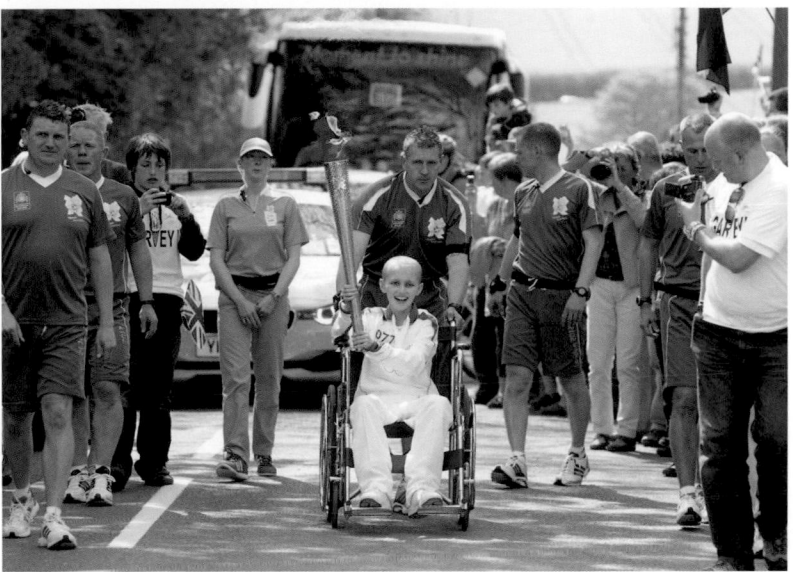

ABOVE: Brave Garvey Evans, 12, takes the Flame through St Stephen, cheered on by the waiting crowds. 'Even though I have been diagnosed with cancer,' Garvey explained, 'I want to be able to inspire people to achieve whatever they want.'

LEFT: Rebecca Cross, 41, a charity fundraiser from Porthowan, passes on the Flame after completing her slot between St Stephen and St Austell. She and her fellow Torchbearer sealed the Torch 'kiss' with a real one on the cheek.

Moment to Shine

Jordan Anderton, 18, evoked a rousing response when he took the Flame through Plymouth. The gifted rugby player was diagnosed with a rare form of childhood cancer. After finishing his treatment he went on to play for the Exeter Chiefs Academy and to start fundraising to support teenagers with cancer. He has raised the profile of the Teenage Cancer Trust and inspired several teams to take part in the Cancer Research Relay for Life, raising tens of thousands of pounds.

Moment to Shine

'I'm just waiting for my Olympic kiss,' joked Jane Allen as she and husband Frank ran their consecutive stints in Torquay, Devon. The Allens were the only married couple in the Relay. Both were nominated for going the extra mile in their community and charitable works – Jane for the Royal Naval Reserve and Royal British Legion; Frank as a contributor to village life and as a weekly swim-buddy for a disabled local man. The Flame was duly transferred from one Torch to another and Jane received a smacker on the cheek.

OPPOSITE: Hats off to Katy Henderson! Torchbearer 050 receives a salute from fellow officer cadets as she begins her leg of the Relay at the Britannia Royal Naval College in Dartmouth, Devon.

ABOVE: Another moment in history for Modbury, Devon. The town mentioned in the Domesday Book greets the Flame with bunting, cameras and festive crowds.

RIGHT: Panoramic views of the Dart Estuary frame the spectacle of the Olympic Torch Relay as it leaves the grounds of the British Royal Naval College, Dartmouth.

ABOVE LEFT: That's the spirit! Alice the British Bulldog waits patiently in patriotic dress for the arrival of the Olympic Flame in Bideford, Devon. Her friend Hugh also shows his colours (behind).

ABOVE RIGHT: Emma Fowler thrills onlookers in Taunton. Photographers, poised on the back of the converted horsebox that is the official media bus, capture the moment as she starts her run.

LEFT: Residents in patriotic headgear share a picnic on the verge as they wait for the Relay to pass through Ilfracombe in Devon.

OPPOSITE: Hip, hip, hooray! Children wave their flags at their roadside 'Little Munchkins Tea Party' as the town of Braunton celebrates the passing of the Torch Relay.

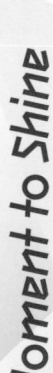

Moment to Shine

Farmer Tony Hill, 86, was due to be a Torchbearer for the 1948 Olympic Games, but had to dash to hospital instead with appendicitis. Hill, a former cross-country runner whose son nominated him with the plea to fulfil his lost dream, said: 'I never thought I'd get another chance. It's been a real honour. I've been doing a bit of jogging to get fit.'

ABOVE: Tiaras for the Torch. Residents of Porlock in Somerset greet the Relay in festive regalia.

RIGHT: Katrina Doyle, 13, carries the Torch uphill through Dunster Castle's medieval arch in Somerset. After battling bravely with childhood leukaemia, she has raised thousands of pounds for charity, including the CLIC Sargent children's cancer charity.

FAR LEFT: Local hero John Saunders, 44, a former feedback engineer at Hinkley Point Power Station, takes the Flame through Folly Gate, on the leg between Okehampton and Merton. He has raised funds for, and enhanced awareness of, Motor Neurone Disease since being diagnosed with the condition in 2010.

LEFT: Olympic gold medallist Jonathan Edwards carries the Olympic Torch on an emotional journey through his home town of Ilfracombe. He took it to show pupils at his former school, West Buckland.

BELOW. Will.i.am, the American rap artist, runs through Taunton prompting the headline of the week – Will.i.ran.

LEFT: Judy Gaden gives the Torch a waterborne start to Day 4 on an electric canal boat along the River Tone in Taunton, Somerset.

ABOVE: Wells Cathedral provides a dramatic backdrop for Torchbearer Anthony Deahl as a member of the Torch security team encourages the cheering crowd. 'I was humbled by the stories of my fellow Torchbearers,' he said.

Travelling in Style

On Day 4 the Olympic Flame took to a canal boat on the River Tone in Taunton. The 6am start did not deter locals from lining the river as Judy Gaden, who lost her son Corporal Tom Gaden in Afghanistan in 2009, carried the Torch on board the Future Perfect electric boat. She was nominated for her charity work, involvement in fundraising for Help for Heroes and for arranging community fun days.

OPPOSITE: Carol Bowery enjoys her moment to shine in the streets of her home town of Bath. She was nominated for supporting young mothers in the community, including helping them gain access to high quality education.

OPPOSITE RIGHT: Air Cadets veteran Tony Bird runs through Wells. A volunteer for the Air Cadets Corps for over 30 years, his motto for his students is, 'If I can do it, you can'.

'There haven't been this many people in Ilchester town centre since they kicked out the Romans.'

Tweet from BBC Somerset's Vernon Harwood

Moment to Shine

Eleanore Regan,
28, was scheduled to run with the Flame while heavily pregnant, but gave birth to William eight days early. The charity worker, who is also battling a brain tumour, ran her 300m through Bath, Somerset, with her tiny baby looking on. Eleanore sets up and runs a variety of charities. In the deprived community of Southmead, Bristol, she runs nutritional cooking classes; in Kenya, she protects new mothers and babies from AIDS; in Eastern Europe she helps young people volunteer and make a difference to their world. 'Like the Olympic Flame, I hope I can pass on light and hope to everyone I work with and meet. Happiness is infectious and my aim is to equip people with the basic things they need in life to be happy - whether it's food, water, shelter, health, friendship, support or community.'

LEFT: A 300m dash uphill in Frome, Somerset, is a walk in the park for John Reynolds, who has run many thousands of miles to raise money for Children's Hospice South West.

OPPOSITE: Natalie Hawkins, 20, from Street in Somerset, stands on top of Glastonbury Tor, an ancient monument believed by some to be the 'Avalon' of Arthurian legend. Now 95 per cent recovered from ME, Natalie's message is that 'sport can heal'.

ABOVE: Karen Horsler, 44, who has overcome chronic back pain that plagued her since childhood to become a marathon runner, enjoys her moment to shine in Brockworth, Gloucestershire.

LEFT: Firework rockets salute Rebecca Pantaney as she carries the Olympic Flame over Brunel's famous Clifton Suspension Bridge in Bristol.

Moment to Shine

Ben Fox,
16, prompted resounding applause and tears of admiration. The wheelchair basketball player, who hopes to compete in the 2016 Paralympic Games, used a crutch for support as he carried the Torch through an emotion-charged Royal Wootton Bassett.

'Just watched 16-year-old Ben Fox carrying the Olympic Torch. Superb determination shown by this young man.'

Tweeted by Jon Preston

LEFT: Ben Fox, 16, was born without a leg, 'but nothing stops him,' said his proud mother Carol Keane. 'He's had a lot to put up with, 32 operations, but he's just an amazing lad … I'm totally overwhelmed. What made today amazing was the fantastic support.'

47

RIGHT: HRH the Princess Royal greets her daughter Zara Phillips and horse Toytown. Zara and Toytown, who retired last year after winning the 2006 Eventing World Championships, carried the Olympic Torch down the finishing straight at Cheltenham Racecourse.

Moment to Shine

Zara Phillips, 31, rode the length of the finishing straight at Cheltenham Racecourse on her horse Toytown to mark the end of Day 5. After trotting past the finishing post to the theme from 'Chariots of Fire', Phillips lit the Cauldron for the evening celebration. 'I'm shaking. It was an unbelievable experience and I am massively honoured for doing it,' she told a cheering audience of more than 30,000. She said participating in the Relay meant Toytown, who missed both the Athens 2004 and Beijing 2008 Games through last-minute injury, could 'do something for the Olympics … This one is for him.' Days later Zara was selected for the Eventing Team Competition.

ABOVE: Paul Watts, a veteran of 217 marathons, takes his turn with the Torch in Hereford. A volunteer at the Royal National College for the Blind and a member of Herefordshire Vision Links, Paul's achievements inspire all who suffer from sight loss.

LEFT: Golden girl Sharron Davies, who won a silver medal in the 1980 Olympic Games, gazes at the Torch before her run in Leominster, Herefordshire. Davies was only 13 years old when she competed for Britain at the 1976 Games in Montreal, and won six Commonwealth Games medals during her career.

'It's been an amazing day. The whole event surprised us – so many people, so many vehicles in the convoy!'

Amber Poole and James Cole

49

ABOVE: All aboard! The guard on the Severn Valley Railway steam train at Bewdley Station prepares to take the Olympic Flame down the line to Kidderminster.

RIGHT: Excited schoolchildren from Bewdley Primary School on board the Worcestershire Express spot the Flame at Bewdley Station.

FAR RIGHT: Torchbearer Christopher Stokes acknowledges the 'trunk salute' from two African elephants at West Midlands Safari Park. Five, aged 20, and Latabe, 19, were trained by wardens at the Safari Park to wave Union flags with their trunks.

Moment to Shine

Gemma Passmore, 28, a specialist paediatric physiotherapist, ran a leg of the Relay in Cardiff. She was nominated as a community champion by her sister for fundraising in the Help for Heroes 'Gym for Heroes' 12-hour non-stop challenge. Dedicated to her profession, Gemnma displays, as her sister says, 'qualities of character that we … should be promoting to the world in 2012'.

ABOVE: Paul Green, deputy manager of the Big Pit in Blaenavon, Wales, is flanked by members of the Olympic Torch security team. A working coal mine from 1860 to 1980, Big Pit was opened to visitors in 1980 as part of the National Museum Wales.

RIGHT: Darren Campbell, a member of Team GB's gold medal-winning 4x100m Relay team at Athens 2004, picks up his latest Relay 'baton' by the river in Worcester.

'The Flame comes to Wales and the volume switch goes up!'

overheard on an overexcited Cardiff High Street

Cardiff Celebrates

The Flame was not due to arrive in central Cardiff until 6.49pm. Yet at 1pm the doors opened at Cooper's Field, a vast green meadow within the picturesque grounds of Cardiff Castle, and the eight-hour city celebration kicked off. It was a great day for the Welsh capital: the sun blazed, locals and visitors milled around or sat on the grass, beers in hand. A festival vibe rocked the city. It started with picnics, gatherings of students and groups of all ages soaking up the buzz provided by live performances from Brit Award winner Emeli Sandé and Cardiff-born act Kids in Glass Houses. Later, many of the day's Torchbearers joined the throng as rock band You Me At Six thrilled a mellow late evening crowd from a stage adorned by the Flame in its Celebration Cauldron.

OPPOSITE: Monmouth schoolchildren wave hands, homemade 'Torches' and flags as they prepare to greet the Relay cavalcade.

ABOVE LEFT: Newport residents use every vantage point to line the route and applaud the Flame's progress. Thousands of people brought towns in Wales to a standstill on Day 7 of the Relay.

BELOW LEFT: Melanie Stephenson, 24, a Welsh runner who suffers from Type 1 diabetes, lights the Cauldron on stage in Cooper's Field after running the last leg with the Olympic Flame through Cardiff.

OVERLEAF: The imminent arrival of the Olympic Flame in front of Wells Cathedral excites the crowd into forming a colourful tunnel to welcome it.

Week 1 Places

SATURDAY Land's End • Sennen • Newlyn • Penzance • Marazion • Rosudgeon • Ashton • Breage • Helston • Falmouth • Truro • Newquay • St Stephen • St Austell • Stenalees • Bugle • Lanivet • Bodmin • Liskeard • Saltash • Plymouth **SUNDAY** Plymouth • Brixton • Yealmpton • Modbury • Kingsbridge • West Charleton • Chillington • Torcross • Stoke Fleming • Dartmouth • Totnes • Paignton • Torquay • Teignmouth • Exeter **MONDAY** Exeter • Okehampton • Folly Gate • Hatherleigh • Merton • Great Torrington • West Bideford • Sticklepath • Barnstaple • Wrafton • Braunton • Knowle • Ilfracombe • Combe Martin • Lynton • Lynmouth • Porlock • Minehead • Dunster • Carhampton • Washford • Williton • Taunton **TUESDAY** Taunton • Ilminster • Yeovil • Ilchester • Somerton • Street • Glastonbury • Coxley • Wells • Croscombe • Shepton Mallet • Frome • Southwick • Trowbridge • Bradford on Avon • Bath • Bitton • Longwell Green • Hanham • Bristol **WEDNESDAY** Bristol • Flax Bourton • Backwell Farleigh • Backwell West Town • Nailsea • Failand • Leigh Woods • Bristol • Chippenham • Calne • Malborough • Chiseldon • Wroughton • Royal Wootton Bassett • Swindon • Cirencester • Stroud • Painswick • Brockworth • Shurdington • Cheltenham **THURSDAY** Gloucester • Maisemore • Hartpury • Corse and Staunton • Ledbury • Bartestree • Lugwardine • Hereford • Leominster • Ludlow • Clee Hill • Cleobury Mortimer • Far Forest • Callow Hill • Bewdley • Kidderminster • Droitwich Spa • Fernhill Heath • Worcester **FRIDAY** Worcester • Powick • Malvern • Malvern Wells • Ross on Wye • Monmouth • Raglan • Abergavenny • Brynmawr • Blaenavon • Abersychan • Pontypool • Newport • Cardiff

Chapter 2
26 May to 1 June

Highlights

Wales – the land of castles and coastlines, dragons and daffodils, history, poetry, coal mines, choirs, rugby and railways – became from 26 May to 29 May the guardian of the London 2012 Olympic Flame. Week 2 action started in Cardiff, fittingly in the hands of a Time Lord: actor Matt Smith, who plays Dr Who. The Relay evoked passionate enthusiasm as it passed through the South Wales Valleys and then turned west to the sea, returning to mid and North Wales and back into northwest England. Red, white and green Welsh flags merged with Union flag banners to form a colourful backdrop of vibrant heritage, local pride and bold endeavour.

Caerphilly Castle, the steelwork city of Port Talbot and the Sail Bridge provided dramatic settings en route to Swansea. In the city a jubilant Ken Bennett, 69, who still holds the Welsh record for the 4 x 1 mile Relay, lit the evening Cauldron in Singleton Park. On

Day 9 it was the turn of rural Wales, with the Flame travelling through the Pembrokeshire Coast National Park and shining on Oystermouth Castle and Kidwelly Castle, setting for the film *Monty Python and the Holy Grail*. Torchbearers ran, grinned, waved, laughed and cried as they were greeted with frenetic flag-waving, car horns, wolf whistles and lively celebration. For good measure, the council in Carmarthen even arranged a giant trampoline to feed the carnival atmosphere.

'Didn't we have a lovely time the day we went to Bangor?' The words of the 1979 hit single matched the sentiment of crowds who witnessed the Flame progress on a cliff-top railway in Aberystwyth and on the Ffestiniog Railway steam train. The itinerary took in Aberystwyth Castle, the Gorsedd Stones and Caernarfon Castle, recalling Prince Charles's investiture as Prince of Wales in 1969. A great day was concluded with theatrical gravitas by Bryn Terfel.

More adventure came the next day, as the Flame sped across the Menai Strait from Anglesey courtesy of an Atlantic 85 RNLI lifeboat. It then ascended Mount Snowdon in the capable hands of mountaineer Sir Chris Bonington, before travelling by cable car to the Great Orme limestone headland. After resting overnight in the Roman city of Chester, where jockey Jason Maguire was the final Torchbearer at the famous Racecourse, the convoy moved to Much Wenlock in Shropshire. Here in 1850 Dr William Penny Brookes founded the Wenlock Olympian Games, giving the town an enduring role in Olympic history. The Games were visited in 1890 by Baron

Pierre de Coubertin, who in turn became inspired to create the global event. Daley Thompson tweeted: 'Olympic Torch in Much Wenlock today u might want to whisper this but the Olympics may have started there in 1850 yes we restarted them.' Umbrellas paid tribute to the British summer on the Stoke to Bolton leg, where Amir Khan was tasked with lighting the Cauldron. 'I think the last boxer to carry a Torch was Muhammad Ali,' Khan observed, 'so this a great honour for me.'

Week 2 ended with a fascinating day centred on Liverpool, starting among the haunting Antony Gormley statues on Crosby Beach. The Flame visited Aintree, where it received a nod from the 2012 Grand National winner Neptune Collonges, and was also greeted by curious giraffes, elephants and 6,000 spectators at the Knowsley Safari Park. Huge crowds gathered to welcome the Flame in front of the iconic Liver Building at the Pier Head. Craig Lundberg, a war veteran who was blinded on duty in Iraq in 2007, had the emotive role of final Torchbearer, transporting the Flame on a ferry across the Mersey from Birkenhead. 'I can't see the pictures, but I can imagine what they look like,' he later noted. 'Our city has the best skyline, the best waterfront and the best people in the world. I only hope I've done them proud.' A crowd of 21,000 turned out to see Lundberg light the Cauldron, as the master of ceremonies announced to deafening applause: 'Liverpool, the Olympic Flame is Yours'. Not a dry eye on the Dock.

PREVIOUS PAGE: Early morning on 29 May sees the Olympic Flame speeding across the Menai Strait from Anglesey with the crew of an Atlantic 85 RNLI lifeboat.

LEFT: Matt Smith, the Dr Who actor, seems humbled by his role as first Torchbearer of the day in Cardiff. 'It's a great honour to run. I would do it in my underpants,' he joked.

Moment to Shine

Early starts don't worry a Time Lord. Doctor Who star Matt Smith was up at dawn to undertake the first leg of the Torch Relay's first full day in Wales. Despite fearing he would be running in front of an audience consisting only of ducks, he was greeted rapturously by a crowd of over a thousand. The actor's run from the historic Norwegian church in Cardiff Bay to the National Assembly building had an amusing resonance for Dr Who fans. In a previous life, the Doctor – then played by David Tennant – had himself travelled forward in time and carried the Olympic Torch in London in 2012.

ABOVE: David Evans, 17, from Barry carries the Flame through Cardiff. He is a passionate badminton player and the youngest qualified national-level umpire in the UK.

FAR RIGHT: Bronwen Davies, 16, nominated for her work raising awareness of climate change, said it was 'amazing' to take the Torch in front of Caerphilly Castle.

RIGHT: Torchbearer Richard Parks sold his house to undertake the 737 challenge (a 7-month race to climb the highest mountain on every continent and reach both Poles) and raise money for Marie Curie Cancer Care. Here he runs along the stunning 142-metre Sail Bridge over the River Tawe in Swansea.

ABOVE: Television presenter Gethin Jones said he was 'too excited' about carrying the Torch through his home town of Merthyr Tydfil. Jones was selected for the honour in recognition of his ongoing support of charitable causes, among them UNICEF, Sport Relief and Haven House Children's Hospice.

LEFT: Spectators scramble to every vantage point, even Dad's shoulders, to spot the Olympic Flame between Caerphilly and Pontypridd.

OPPOSITE: Philip Richards, nominated for his work in South Wales Special Constabulary, brandishes the Olympic Torch on top of Oystermouth Castle, overlooking Swansea Bay.

'It was an honour to carry such an iconic symbol just down the street from where I was born.'

Gethin Jones, TV presenter, on running with the Torch in Merthyr Tydfil

'It's like a massive street party everywhere we go with the Torch.'

A member of the South Wales Police team escort

RIGHT: Jill Edge decorated her mobility scooter with flags and the Olympic rings to give the Flame a fitting chariot for its journey through Fishguard. Jill, who has had a progressive arthritic condition since her teens, campaigns for rights for disabled people and has helped save two local theatres from closure.

BELOW: Paul Adams, an inspiring cyclist, waves to watching crowds as he takes the Olympic Flame aboard the Swansea Bay Rider. The 72-seater train runs on the promenade between Blackpill and Southend.

Eric Davies rides his 12-year-old bay mare, Maesmynach Angerdd, through Aberaeron in the county of Ceredigion – widely regarded as 'Welsh cob country' because of the long history of cob breeding in the area.

Travelling in Style

Hardy, sure-footed, intelligent and with an excellent temperament, the Ceredigion Cob Horse had its moment to shine as a breed. Eric Davies, President of the Welsh Pony and Cob Society, carried the Torch from the saddle of his 12-year-old, 15.3 hands-high mare Maesmynach Angerdd (Welsh for passion) in Aberaeron. 'It's a great honour to be carrying the Olympic Flame, not just for me but for the Welsh Cob and its roots as a breed in Ceredigion,' he enthused. Semi-feral Welsh Cobs are said to have roamed the mountains since 1600 BC. Throughout history, they have been put to many uses: on postal routes, in coal mines, for mounted infantry or for pulling heavy guns and equipment for the British War Office, and as beloved riding ponies for both children and adults.

Moment to Shine

Elin Davies,
35, ran with the Flame in Bangor. Elin, a nurse, has raised nearly £250,000 for charities by rowing 9,159km across two of the world's oceans. She landed in Antigua to become the first Welsh woman ever to row across the Atlantic Ocean. Fourteen months later, Elin joined team 'Ocean Angels', with whom she set a world record becoming the first all-female crew to row 5,052km across the Indian Ocean. The crew took 78 days, 15 hours and 54 minutes.

ABOVE: The sun shines and the crowd cheers on Peter Pearse, Head Coach for Boccia Wales since 2007 and Team GB's Performance Coach, as he travels with the Olympic Flame through Caernarfon on the leg between Bontnewydd and Y Felinheli.

RIGHT: Bridget James holds the Olympic Flame at the National Library of Wales in Aberystwyth. Bridget and her husband aimed to raise over £8,000 for the four charities that supported them following the early birth of their first daughter with congenital heart problems. Bridget has so inspired people to run marathons, climb mountains and cycle across nations that, less than halfway through the appeal, their target was smashed three times over.

ABOVE LEFT: PC Andrew Thomas, one of the 35-strong Metropolitan Police Torch Security Team, aka 'the Runners', escorts the Olympic Flame in a Lantern during its journey along the Ffestiniog Railway to Porthmadog.

ABOVE RIGHT: Another 'kiss' for the Olympic Flame, symbolic of peace, unity and friendship, as it progresses along its 70-day, 8,000-strong human chain.

LEFT: Secure in its Lantern, the Flame travels in a steam engine on the narrow gauge Ffestiniog Railway. The 13½-mile route features pastures and forests, lakes and waterfalls, as it runs from the slate-quarrying town of Blaenau Ffestiniog to the harbour in Porthmadog.

Moment to Shine

Sir Chris Bonington
The Torch Relay reached new emotional heights when the Olympic Flame travelled to the summit of Mount Snowdon, the highest point in the British Isles outside Scotland and the legendary burial place of the giant ogre Rhita, vanquished by King Arthur. At 9.10am, the Flame set off on the Snowdon Mountain Railway, carried in its Lantern for safety. Travelling with it was the distinguished mountaineer Sir Chris Bonington, who clambered through the crowds to the very top with his lit Torch. The clouds parted and he stood, arms aloft, with the Flame silhouetted against the sky. 'It exceeded all my dreams and expectations,' said Sir Chris, who used to train on Snowdon. 'It was a combination of firstly having the great honour of carrying the Torch up to the top of Snowdon, but also the fact that this is part – and perhaps coming towards the end – of a long personal journey which started when I was 16. Today is so much to do with my climbing heritage. This mountain still grips me.'

RIGHT: Lorna Price, nominated for overcoming her visual impairment to compete in karate and gymnastics, starts Day 11 of the Relay on the Isle of Anglesey at Beaumaris Castle.

FAR RIGHT: On a winning streak. Grand National-winning jockey Jason Maguire rides Overturn, a horse trained by Donald McCain Jr, after lighting the Cauldron in front of a crowd of over 25,000 at Chester Racecourse.

BELOW: The Olympic Flame enjoys life on the ocean wave in the Atlantic 85 inshore lifeboat *Annette Mary Liddington*. The Flame was escorted on the 15-minute voyage from Anglesey to the North Wales mainland by a selection of the RNLI's fleet on the Menai Strait.

RIGHT: Olympic gymnast Beth Tweddle takes over Relay duties as the Olympic Flame reached the Welsh border, carrying the Torch through her home town of Saltney en route to Chester. 'This is not just for me, or my supporters; it's for all of Saltney so they feel part of the Olympic Games,' she declared.

BELOW: Jay Lusted carries the Olympic Flame on the leg between Llandudno and his home town of Colwyn Bay. His nomination story describes him as 'an inspirational individual who has overcome a number of difficulties … he has never once believed that he has a disability but has many abilities to inspire others through his passion for sport, religion and life. Badminton is not a Paralympic discipline but if it was, he would be there in London representing Team GB in 2012.'

Moment to Shine

Jay Lusted, 24, from Colwyn Bay, who brought the Olympic Flame through Rhos-on-Sea, stands three foot seven inches tall, but is described by the person who nominated him as having 'the personality, charisma and passion of a man 10 times his size' as he encourages others to become involved in disability sport. He is a keen badminton player and has won the Welsh Junior Sports Personality award three years in a row.

'I went out to see the Torch in Telford … It was a lovely childlike experience for me. I was not a parent, husband, granddad or anything like that. For the 20 minutes of the experience, I was just me.'

Peter Nottle

LEFT: Residents of Much Wenlock celebrate as they await the arrival of the Olympic Flame. The Shropshire town, site of the Wenlock Olympian Games founded by Dr William Penny Brookes in 1850, can claim to be the birthplace of the modern event. Baron Pierre de Coubertin was inspired by the Wenlock Olympian Games, which he visited, and Wenlock, one of the London 2012 official mascots, is named after the town.

BELOW: Local schoolchildren in Wrexham wave Welsh banners and Union flags as they throng the route to welcome the Olympic Flame.

Travelling in Style

Question: How can the Olympic Flame both take to the water and be 126ft up in the air?
Answer: When it travelled with Torchbearer Joanne Gregory on a barge, pulled along by four volunteer members of the Shropshire Union Fly-boat Restoration Society, dressed in 19th-century costume, across the Pontcysyllte Aqueduct. The landmark is a navigable aqueduct that carries the Llangollen Canal over the valley of the River Dee in Wrexham in northeast Wales. Completed in 1805, it is the longest and highest aqueduct in Britain, a Grade I Listed Building and a UNESCO World Heritage Site.

OPPOSITE: Four volunteer members of the Shropshire Union Fly-boat Restoration Society wear 19th-century costume as they hand-pull the barge bearing the Olympic Flame, carried by Joanne Gregory, along the Pontcysllte Aqueduct and Llangollen Canal in Trevor.

ABOVE: Imran Sherwani, a Team GB Hockey gold medallist from the 1988 Seoul Games, ignites the crowd and the Cauldron at Hanley Park in Stoke-on-Trent.

RIGHT: Dimitrios Eforakopoulos thrills supporters of the Olympic spirit in Much Wenlock. He has attended all the official Olympic lighting ceremonies since 1972 and served as a Torchbearer in the Athens 2004 Olympic Torch Relay. 'I feel very proud to participate one more time,' he said.

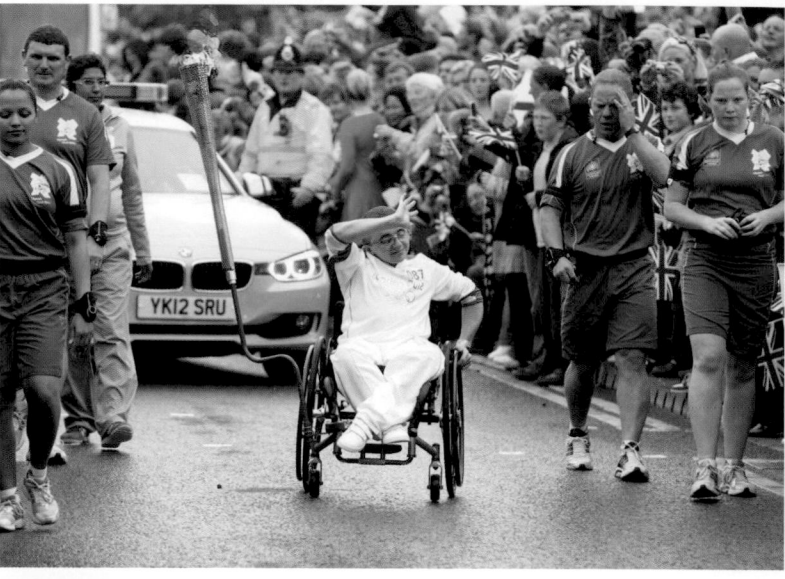

ABOVE LEFT: Torchbearers Cyril Baker and Jazmin Sawyers link arms in a jubilant dance to mark the handover of the Flame. 'Jazmin was just fab, buzzing, she made my day. So excited, interacting with the crowd and just loving her moment,' commented one onlooker in Congleton.

LEFT: Amir Khan, who became Britain's youngest Olympic Boxing medallist when he won silver at the 2004 Athens Games, proudly runs the final leg of the day. Khan took the Flame into Queen's Park to light the Celebration Cauldron at the evening event hosted by his home town of Bolton.

ABOVE: Damp summer weather does not deter the thousands of spectators thronging the streets and applauding Daniel Dawoud's journey with the Olympic Flame.

OPPOSITE: Kimberley Cooper, accompanied by 2012 Grand National winner Neptune Collonges (resplendent in a London 2012 horse blanket), shares the Olympic Flame with the crowds who flocked to the racecourse at Aintree.

'You just get carried away with it. Everyone is having such a good time. It's brilliant.'

Kimberley Cooper, Torchbearer 084, at Aintree

ABOVE: Jane Campbell, 36, a community activist dedicated to supporting senior citizens, greets a hungry giraffe after completing her 300m stretch through Knowsley Safari Park.

FAR LEFT: Jessica Wade, 14, stands as still as a statue at Another Place, Antony Gormley's haunting art installation at Crosby Beach, Liverpool. Jessica was selected for her triathlon and Swimathon efforts in aid of Animals in Need.

LEFT: Dogged determination. Winston the Bulldog sports a Union flag party hat in the village of Euxton, near Chorley in Lancashire.

'I'm on top of the world. It's great that I am representing the city. And what an iconic scene, to be on the ferry going over to Liverpool.'

War veteran Craig Lundberg describes bringing the Flame across the Mersey at the end of a dramatic day

LEFT: Craig Lundberg, a war veteran who lost his sight on duty in Iraq in 2007, represents the city of Liverpool as he takes a ferry across the Mersey en route to the evening celebration on Liverpool's Pier Head. 'I only hope I've done them proud,' he said.

BELOW LEFT: The Olympic Flame burns brightly in the Cauldron below the iconic skyline of the Royal Liver Building, home to two fabled Liver Birds that watch over the city and the sea.

OVERLEAF: Against a glorious summer evening sky, a large and passionate crowd decked out in red, white and blue waits outside the Liver Building for the stirring moment when Craig Lundberg is guided up on stage to light the Cauldron. Huge cheers greeted the booming announcement: 'Liverpool, the Olympic Flame is Yours.'

Week 2 Places

SATURDAY Cardiff • Dinas Powys • Barry • Caerphilly • Pontypridd • Merthyr Tydfil • Treherbert • Ynyswen • Treorchy • Nant-y-moel • Ogmore Vale • Bryncethin • Bridgend • Laleston • Pyle • Margam • Taibach • Port Talbot • Briton Ferry • Neath • Swansea **SUNDAY** Swansea • Llanelli • Burry Port • Kidwelly • Carmarthen • Haverfordwest • Fishguard • Newport • Cardigan/Aberteifi • Sarnau • Brynhoffnant • Llanarth • Aberaeron • Llanon • Llanrhystud • Aberystwyth **MONDAY** Aberystwyth • Bow Street • Tal-y-bont • Tre Taliesin • Machynlleth • Dolgellau • Llan Ffestiniog • Blaenau Ffestiniog • Porthmadog • Criccieth • Pwllheli • Bontnewydd • Caernarfon • Y Felinheli • Bangor **TUESDAY** Beaumaris • Menai Bridge • Conwy • Deganwy • Llandudno • Penrhyn Bay • Rhos on Sea • Colwyn Bay • Old Colwyn • Abergele • Towyn • Kinmel Bay • Rhyl • Rhuddlan • Connah's Quay • Shotton • Queensferry • Harwarden • Saltney • Chester **WEDNESDAY** Chester • Wrexham • Rhostyllen • Acrefair • Trevor • Oswestry • Pant • Llanymynech • Welshpool • Shrewsbury • Cressage • Much Wenlock • Benthall • Broseley • Ironbridge • Telford • Newport • Gnosall • Haughton • Stafford • Shelton • Stoke on Trent **THURSDAY** Stoke on Trent • Cobridge • Burslem • Middleport • Crewe • Congleton • Macclesfield • Knutsford • Runcorn • Widnes • Warrington • Lowton • Abram • Wigan • Scholes • Ince • Hindley • Westhoughton • Bolton **FRIDAY** Bolton • Horwich • Chorley • Euxton • Croston • Burscough • Ormskirk • Southport • Ainsdale • Formby • Crosby • St Helen's • Huyton • Knotty Ash • Old Swan • Liverpool • Birkenhead • Liverpool

Chapter 3
2 to 8 June

Highlights

From Liverpool, the Flame flew to the Isle of Man in BA2012 'The Firefly', the gold-liveried plane that had brought it from Greece to the UK, where it was treated to several speedy modes of transport. The first came courtesy of a TT motorbike, with three-time World Enduro Champion David Knight riding pillion behind former TT winner Richard 'Milky' Quayle. The Flame proceeded to whoosh down the ramp of the Douglas RNLI station, before trundling past fairgrounds on a horse tram, going on a bike ride along the promenade and taking a trip on the Manx Electric Railway. A pause from the whirlwind action came at the 22m-tall Laxey Wheel, the largest working waterwheel in the world.

Then the Flame boarded 'The Firefly' once again for a flight on to Belfast, where Day 16 began at a newly opened museum, Titanic Belfast. Standing on the slipways where the RMS Titanic was built, the Relay's presence gave a poignant nod to the centenary of the famous ship's sinking. The party spirit quickly returned in Belfast's streets, thronged with delighted onlookers – some wearing dressing gowns, others carrying 'keep 'er lit' signs!

The Flame then moved to Bangor and back via Stormont, the seat of the Northern Ireland Assembly, and Belfast Zoo, where it was welcomed by a sea lion. Brass bands and barbecue aromas warmed spirits in the icy cold as the convoy passed Carrickfergus Castle and continued up the coast to Ballycastle, famous for its seaweed and honeycomb treats.

The morning of Day 17 was devoted to landmarks: Carrick-a-Rede Rope Bridge, the famous Giant's Causeway and the cliff-top Dunluce Castle. The Torch glinted against an azure sky as it was rowed merrily along the River Bann, and a buzzing party in St Columb's Park, Derry, reverberated around the only completely walled city in the UK.

Another day, another audio visual feast. The Relay departed from Derry's Peace Bridge for Newry via Omagh and Enniskillen, the most westerly point of its journey. Enniskillen introduced straw-masked 'mummers' and Armagh released a mass of blue balloons. Marble Arch Caves displayed its underworld 'bunting' of magnificent stalactites. In Portadown umbrellas went up, as did the decibel levels for a jubilant celebration at Newry's Pairc Esler.

The Relay then made a significant departure from the UK as it crossed the border en route to Dublin. Offices and schools emptied, and surgeons in scrubs were seen on pavements taking pictures as the Flame flickered over Samuel Beckett Bridge, before heading past St Patrick's and Christ Church Cathedrals, Dublin Castle and Government Buildings. Michael Ring TD, Minister of State for Tourism and Sport, paid tribute to 'the friendship, peace

Meeting in the middle: Clare Leahy and Denis Broderick let their Torches 'kiss' above a 30m deep chasm on the Carrick-a-Rede Rope Bridge when the Torch Relay explored the coast of County Antrim. The rocky island offers magnificent views across the sea to Scotland.

and cooperation that now exists on the island of Ireland and demonstrates the unifying power of sport'. Champion jump jockey Ruby Walsh wished horse racing was an Olympic sport ('Ireland would clean up!!') and pop duo Jedward Flame-kissed with former footballer 'Ooh ah, Paul McGrath'.

Back in Northern Ireland, the Flame zigzagged through 13 communities before embarking for Stranraer on the ferry from Larne to begin its Scottish tour. Comedian Patrick Kielty whipped up spectators in his hometown of Dundrum with an Irish dance. A boat trip across Lough Neagh, the largest freshwater lake in the British Isles, was a midday highlight.

By 5.30am on Day 21, the biggest yet dawn crowd sent the Olympic Flame off on its eight-day tour of Scotland with first-day homages paid at Robert Burns's birthplace, Hampden Park and Kelvingrove Art Gallery. Bagpipes skirled, multi-coloured flags fluttered and school orchestras set up on roadsides. Actor James McAvoy, Olympic rower Katherine Grainger and Olympic gold medallist curler Rhona Martin proudly paraded the Flame in Glasgow towards a spirited celebration in George Square.

FAR LEFT: The flickering Olympic Flame fascinates Ian Williams, Rugby Development Officer and head coach of the Isle of Man U18s Rugby Sevens team, on his leg between Laxey and Castletown.

ABOVE LEFT: A precious cargo. Paul Deighton, Chief Executive of LOCOG, carries the Olympic Flame off BA2012 'The Firefly' after its flight from Liverpool to the Isle of Man.

LEFT: When in Rome… David Knight, a three-time World Enduro Champion, introduces the Olympic Flame to TT racing as he rides pillion behind Richard Quayle through Douglas, capital of the Isle of Man.

OPPOSITE: James Holmes, 13, from 1st Arbory Scouts, relishes his Olympic Torch Relay experience. Crowds thronged South Quay, Douglas, to see the Torch take a ride on RNLI Lifeboat Sir William Hillary.

'It looked beautiful as the Flame came round Douglas Quay. RNLI Relay quite moving.'

Tweeted by Christine Mitchell

Moment to Shine

Emily Dale-Beeton, 12, an elite gymnast from Peel, Isle of Man, carried the Torch through Douglas on Day 15. Emily, who was the youngest member of the Youth Commonwealth Games team in 2011, trains over 18 hours a week. Despite the long hours, her nomination story notes that 'she never complains … even when she has the chance of a day off she goes to the gym to train.' Always willing to help younger gymnasts when they ask for help, 'she has learnt to push herself to be a better person through her sport'. 'I want to make it to the Olympic Games and I look forward to it every single day,' she said before her Torch Relay slot.

ABOVE: Maureen Barnes-Sherring, 73, an instructor for Riding for the Disabled for nearly 40 years, gives the Olympic Flame a gentle outing on a Horse Tram. Delighted crowds festooned with flags lined the promenade between Douglas and Laxey.

RIGHT: 'Keep 'er lit' was the slogan adopted by the Irish crowds. Here the Olympic Flame goes into safekeeping mode, transferring from a Torch into a Lantern as it travelled on the Manx Electric Railway.

ABOVE: Geraldine McCann, an ambassador for cancer awareness and an advocate of exercise for all ages, is well known in her local community of Lurgan for charity work. She gamely ran uphill to take the Flame on to the steps of Stormont.

LEFT: Michael Rea, 18, enjoys a moment with the Olympic Torch and a California Sea Lion at Belfast Zoo. He was selected as a Torchbearer for his ambition to become an environment-enhancing architect.

'It was such a surreal moment, running up the steps of Stormont with the Olympic Torch. It was just unbelievable.'

Geraldine McCann, Torchbearer 038, from Lurgan

Moment to Shine

Kylie Watson

From enemy firepower to a friendly Flame. Kylie Watson, a 25-year-old army medic from Ballymena, won the Military Cross for twice risking her life under heavy fire to treat two soldiers in Afghanistan. Kylie is only the fourth woman to receive the honour, which is awarded in recognition of exemplary gallantry during active operations against the enemy on land. She carried the Flame through Portrush.

RIGHT: In Portrush, Brendan Duddy, 76, a talented athlete who ran every day until he suffered a stroke in May 2010, carries the Olympic Flame. His commitment to peace and encouragement of sport for all have made him an inspirational figure in his community.

BELOW: Torchbearer Lisa Hickson displays the Torch outside Carrickfergus Castle. The principal of Kircubbin Community Nursery School, her Torchbearer role thrilled her daughter who nominated her for being the 'best mummy'.

'A man just cycled past holding up a lit lighter. Ah, good old NI craic!'

Tweet from Tina Arean

ABOVE: Siun Heaney, 17, who helped design the Northern Ireland Olympic mascot pin badge, passes the Hands across the Divide bronze sculpture in Derry. The sculpture, designed by Derry teacher Maurice Harron, symbolises the spirit of reconciliation and hope for the future.

ABOVE RIGHT: Jean Jones, who cares for a daughter with special needs, holds the Olympic Torch aloft in front of the medieval ruins of Dunluce Castle.

RIGHT: Seamus Reynolds, head coach at Bann Rowing Club, has inspired many Ulster oarsmen including current Team GB Olympian sculler Alan Campbell. He carried the Olympic Flame on an eight-man coxed rowing boat down the River Bann.

Giant's Causeway

The Olympic Flame added a new layer of myth to the story of Giant's Causeway, a UNESCO World Heritage Site made up of 40,000 large black basalt hexagonal columns which protrude from the sea. The distinctive columns were formed when molten rock was forced up through fissures in the earth and then rapidly cooled. However, legend claims the causeway was created during a dispute between a local warrior hero, Finn McCool, and a Scottish giant, Benandonner. When the Scottish giant came across the pathway, Finn disguised himself as a baby in a cot, thus fooling Benandonner into thinking that if the son were so huge, the father must be enormous – and he fled, tearing up the Causeway as he went.

One man and his Torch. Peter Jack, a veteran of Ironman triathlons, provides hundreds of photo-album memories as he holds the Olympic Flame aloft against a perfect blue sky on the Giant's Causeway. 'It was an amazing feeling to turn around and wave at the crowd once I made it to the top,' he said. 'What a fantastic crowd and a fantastic day!'

Carrick-a-Rede

Carrick-a-Rede is a tiny island which is reached by a rope bridge over a 30m deep chasm. The location, which is owned by the National Trust, is a Site of Special Scientific Interest for its unique geology, flora and fauna. The Olympic Flame was taken onto the bridge by Clare Leahy whose Torch 'kissed' that of Denis Broderick.

'The whole day's been special ... you could come to Coleraine and the coast 100 days a year and not get a day like this.'

Denis Broderick, who carried the Torch over Carrick-a-Rede rope bridge

ABOVE LEFT: After a lifelong pursuit of various sports Denis Broderick, 65, continues with the motto 'We don't stop playing because we are old: we get old because we stop playing'. He passed the Olympic Flame to Clare Leahy on the famous Carrick-a-Rede Rope Bridge, originally constructed by salmon fishermen so they could check their nets.

LEFT: Ella-Rose Sainsbury, 12, the first girl to play in her school football team in 15 years, and Mark Horton, 32, who sets up charitable projects to improve the quality of rivers, exchange a Torch 'kiss' on Downhill Beach in Londonderry.

ABOVE: Head over heels... Ewan McAteer, 12, dreams of being the first male gymnast from Northern Ireland to represent his country at the Olympic Games. He performs a backflip in Portadown after passing the Flame to Ulster Schools athletics champion Sarah Moore.

LEFT: Come on Team GB! Spectators show their patriotic fervour as the Torch Relay proceeds from Fivemiletown to Aughnacloy.

'Just watching the Torch going through Armagh! Coat on, brolly up, let's go and see history!'

Tweet from Jonathan Harper

Moment to Shine

Amanda Rice, 34, carried the Flame through Banbridge. After having a near-fatal car crash which left her bedridden for six months, she pushed herself emotionally and physically to learn to walk again. Amanda has also overcome cervical cancer. Since then she has won a bronze medal in her first ever world kickboxing championships, representing Northern Ireland, in 2010. As her nominator wrote: 'If you're looking for someone inspirational, she's your gal – small town girl who dares to dream big, gets knocked down, but gets up stronger every time.'

ABOVE: Woodwind and brass players of St Eugene's band, founded in 1884, serenade the Olympic Flame through Omagh.

LEFT: No hands! Police outriders support a man wobbling on a unicycle behind the 4mph Olympic Torch Relay convoy as it journeys through Omagh.

Border Crossing

On Day 19, the Flame left the United Kingdom for a few hours to travel to Dublin. Just before 7am at Carrickarnon, on the former main Belfast-to-Dublin road, the Olympic Flame crossed the border in the hands of two of Ireland's Olympic boxers: silver medal winning Wayne McCullough and gold medal winning Michael Carruth. As McCullough, 41, kissed the head of Carruth, 44, their bond was a fitting reflection of the symbolism of the Olympic Flame. McCullough is from the Protestant Shankill Road in Belfast while Carruth is a Catholic from Dublin; both represented Ireland in the 1992 Barcelona Olympic Games.

'To cross the Border is a big thing, a big step,' noted McCullough. 'Boxing was always a sport where Catholic and Protestant came together, nobody brought them together, they came together themselves. I'm honoured to be passing on the Flame.'

OPPOSITE: John Collins, a member of the Torch Security Team, escorts the Olympic Flame in a Lantern through the fascinating underworld of rivers in the Marble Arch Caves Global Geopark. Straddling the border between Northern Ireland and the Republic of Ireland just outside Enniskillen, it was one of the first Geoparks to be designated in Europe.

'This is history right here.'

Wayne McCullough

Moment to Shine

Andrea Bingham, 37, from Belfast donated a kidney to her son Ben whose own kidneys were irrevocably damaged before birth. In order to donate, Andrea had to lose three stone. As a coach at Abbey Judo Club at the Valley Leisure Centre, Newtonabbey, she started competing again. In the process she not only lost the weight, but also became Northern Ireland Senior Champion and won a silver medal in the NI Open and a bronze in the Scottish Open. Ben had the life-changing transplant operation soon after his fifth birthday, and will compete in the UK Transplant Games this year.

ABOVE: Olympian Ronnie Delany, who won a gold medal in the 1500m at the 1956 Melbourne Games, poses outside Government Buildings in Dublin with the Olympic Flame and Bridget Taylor, mother of boxer Katie Taylor.

RIGHT: Inside Croke Park, the HQ of the Gaelic Athletic Association, Henry Shefflin holds the Olympic Flame. One of the most decorated players in Gaelic games history, he went on to parade it gingerly from the 40m heights of the new Skyline walkway above the great stadium.

OPPOSITE: 'Oooh aah Paul McGrath': the familiar football chant greets the retired Republic of Ireland international defender as he jogs over the Samuel Beckett Bridge in Dublin. McGrath is widely recognised as one of the best footballers ever to come out of Ireland, playing for Manchester United and Aston Villa during his 17-year career.

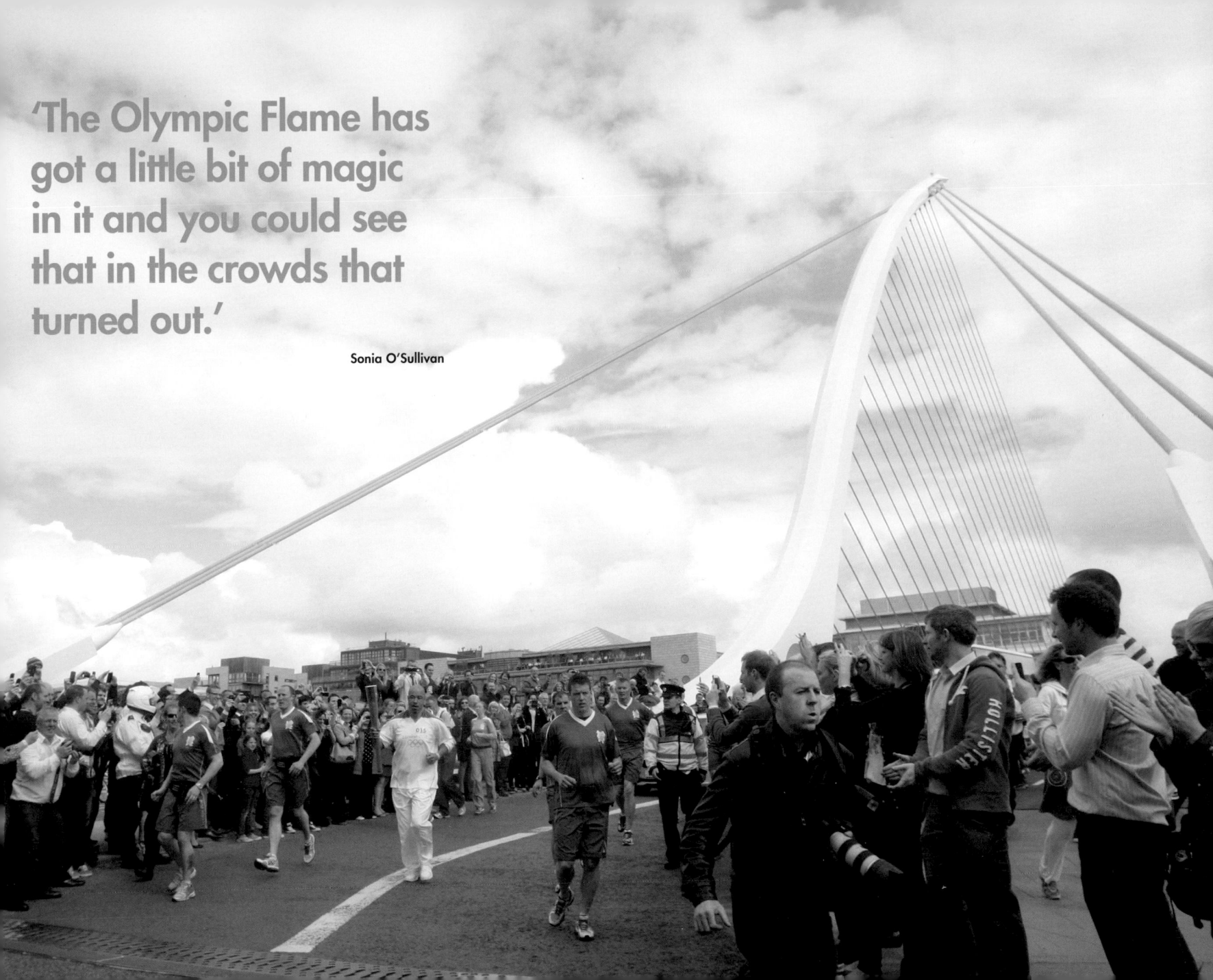

'The Olympic Flame has got a little bit of magic in it and you could see that in the crowds that turned out.'

Sonia O'Sullivan

ABOVE LEFT: A jubilant young Torchbearer poses for pictures with his friends as the Olympic Flame visits Antrim Forum Sports Centre. Six countries – Ireland, Kuwait, Sudan, Egypt, Qatar and Jordan – used the Borough as a training camp for London 2012.

ABOVE RIGHT: Young spectators wear ponchos to protect themselves from the showers as they wait for the Flame to pass through Ballyronan.

LEFT: Eorann Oneill, 16, carries the Flame over the waters of Lough Neagh. A member of the Irish water polo team, she is 'a finger length away from being on the Ulster Swimming Squad' and aims for the Olympic Games one day.

Moment to Shine

Zoe Salmon, former Blue Peter presenter, carried the Flame to Antrim Forum. Zoe, a law graduate and former Miss Northern Ireland, from Bangor, had an adventurous time on the BBC children's show: she ran the London Marathon, raced in a Formula One car, walked on fire and trekked to the top of the UK's highest peaks. She has supported the Tickled Pink breast cancer charity for several years and is an ongoing supporter of the 2012 Sports Relief campaign.

LEFT: Flame dance: comedian Patrick Kielty encourages spectators to join him in an Irish dance as he jigs through his home town of Dundrum. It was an emotional moment for Kielty who later revealed: 'The minute the Torch was put in my hand someone whispered in my ear "You're doing Dundrum proud and your dad would have been very proud, off you go".'

ABOVE: Awestruck young children wave their striking homemade Olympic 'Torches', wrought from metallic paper and flame-coloured tissue, as they watch the Relay pass by in Templepatrick.

'Ayr is the town of honest men and bonnie lasses and it looks like they've all turned out for the Torch. Quite unbelievable crowds.'

Willie Johnston, BBC Scotland

ABOVE LEFT: Ross McClelland, 6'5" and 20 years of age, gives the Flame a towering ride on its first day in Scotland. Ross, an infantry soldier from Ayr, was nominated by his brother: 'Ross loves every minute of his military service although it is extremely demanding. One of his dreams is to become a long-distance runner and compete in the Olympic Games.'

ABOVE RIGHT: Scottish actor James McAvoy – star of 'The Chronicles of Narnia', 'The Last King of Scotland', 'Atonement' and 'X-Men' – gives the Olympic Flame a superhero run down a thronged Buchanan Street in his native Glasgow.

OPPOSITE: The Olympic Torch Relay passes Robert Burns Cottage, the birthplace of the Ayrshire ploughman who became Scotland's national bard and one of the world's best known poets.

OVERLEAF: Wheelie good fun. The Laxey Wheel on the Isle of Man, visited on Day 15 of the Torch Relay, was built in 1854 by a local engineer to pump water from the Laxey mines. With its diameter of 22.1m and speed of three revolutions per minute, Laxey is the largest working waterwheel in the world.

Week 3 Places

SATURDAY Liverpool • Douglas • Laxey • Onchan • Ballasalla • Castletown **SUNDAY** Belfast • Holywood • Bangor • Newtownards • Comber • Dundonald • Stormont • Newtownabbey • Carrickfergus • Glynn • Larne • Drains Bay • Ballygally • Glenarm • Carnlough • Glenariff • Cushendall • Ballycastle • Dervock • Bushmills • Portrush **MONDAY** River Bann • Coleraine • Articlave • Castlerock • Downhill • Bellarena • Limavady • Ballykelly • Greysteel • Derry **TUESDAY** Derry • New Buildings • Magheramason • Bready • Ballymagorry • Strabane • Sion Mills • Omagh • Dromore • Irvinestown • Enniskillen • Fivemiletown • Clogher • Augher • Aughnacloy • Caledon • Armagh • Portadown • Gilford • Banbridge • Newry **WEDNESDAY** Newry • Lisburn • Belfast **THURSDAY** Newcastle • Dundrum • Clough • Downpatrick • Crossgar • Saintfield • Ballynahinch • Templepatrick • Antrim • Ballyronan • Magherafelt • Ballymena • Moorfields **FRIDAY** Stranraer • Cairnryan • Ballantrae • Girvan • Turnberry • Maidens • Kirkoswald • Maybole • Alloway • Ayr • Kilmarnock • Kilmaurs • Stewarton • Dunlop • Barrmill • Beith • Lochwinnoch • Kilmacolm • Port Glasgow • Rutherglen • Glasgow • Giffnock • Glasgow

Chapter 4
9 to 15 June

Highlights

A piper played 'Scotland the Brave' as the Olympic Flame set off from the tall ship The Glenlee, on the River Clyde in Glasgow, to Inverness, greeted by crowds amassed at Loch Lomond and Loch Ness. Drivers who were stuck on the only road in and out of the Highlands happily whipped out their cameras. The beautiful landscape stole the show as the Flame crossed the snow-capped Highlands, ascended by ski lift to the Nevis Centre and tested Loch Ness by boat. Inverness showed lively support as peals of church bells launched their evening celebration.

Day 23 saw the Torch Relay depart for its northernmost destinations: Kirkwall, the capital of Orkney, and Lerwick in the Shetland Islands. St Magnus Cathedral was the magnet for locals to witness the Flame as it embarked on a double loop around Kirkwall (inspiring a double-sided banner: 'Morna is my hero'/ 'Helen is my hero' for the relevant lap). In a nod to the heritage of the bleak and beautiful Shetlands, the Flame travelled on a yoal, or Norwegian longboat, and was welcomed by a Viking guard of honour, to deafening cheers from children resplendent in woolly hats to combat the wind. The Flame then flew to the Isle of Lewis and visited John O'Groats.

Monday 11 June marked the longest journey of the Torch Relay: 400 miles from the Isle of Lewis to Aberdeen. The Callanish Standing Stones on Stornoway in the Western Isles provided a stunning setting for sunrise, witnessed by 75 hardy souls and a lone piper in a specially woven gold and white tweed. The Flame enjoyed a special escort courtesy of a shinty team, a turn on a quad bike and a spectacular Stornoway send-off before flying on to Inverness where a crowd had assembled at the Castle beneath the statue of Flora MacDonald. Next stop was Aviemore, then Crathie, amid glorious scenery in Royal Deeside, home of Balmoral Castle. Appreciative cheers from the 'Granite City' of Aberdeen, where golfer Colin Montgomerie strode out with a grin, fuelled the convoy towards Dundee via Scone Palace. The opening scene of 'Chariots of Fire' was re-enacted on West Sands Beach in St Andrews, with Torchbearer Joseph Forrester, aged 13, leading students from Madras College along the seashore.

Stirling Castle, the Wallace Monument and the famous Forth Bridge provided dramatic settings as the Relay journeyed on to Edinburgh. More than 50,000 people lined the streets of the Scottish capital, where giant Olympic rings on the Mound focused the city's expectation. They gave a huge roar of applause to Sally Hyder when, having carried the Torch in her wheelchair with her assistance dog Harmony, she stood up to walk the last few yards of her stretch.

Allan Wells, 100m gold medallist at the 1980 Olympic Games in Moscow, was among the Torchbearers, running a leg in Selkirk. Chris Paterson, at 34 Scotland's most capped rugby player with 109 appearances, took the Flame in Galashiels, where balloons in Olympic colours were released. Chirnside produced the largest home-made 'Torch' yet, and in Banchory flower petals were strewn into the path of a Torchbearer using a wheelchair.

The convoy headed through the Borders, crossing into England north of Berwick-upon-Tweed and weaving along the castle-studded coastline of Northumbria. Magic was in the air as the Relay approached Alnwick Castle, better known as Hogwarts in the Harry Potter films. At 7.20pm on 14 June, the Olympic Cauldron was lit in Alnwick Castle Pastures, with Lewis Denny, 16, a young actor and fundraiser, completing the lighting honours. He admitted that he was shaking with the drama of it all. 'And I know my mam will be out there, crying,' he said.

On Day 27, the Torch Relay travelled down to Newcastle for a traditionally warm welcome. Crowds greeting Geordie hero and 1966 World Cup winner Jack Charlton, aged 77, brought the city centre to a standstill in the sunshine, after which Chief Scout Bear Grylls took Week 4 to a spectacular climax. The adventurer whizzed the Flame by zip wire from the Tyne Bridge, thrilling thousands of cheering spectators. 'It was amazing,' Grylls said after his 400m slide, having made a safe landing in the parade ground of HMS Calliope.

Da na na na na na, da na na na na! Onlookers hum the ubiquitously played 'Chariots of Fire' theme tune as Joseph Forrester, aged 13, runs with the Torch along West Sands beach in St Andrews in a re-enactment of the film's iconic opening scene.

'If there was ever a time for Nessie to make an appearance – it is now!'

Chris Meads

RIGHT: Blair Marquis, a former Northern Constabulary Officer, was nominated as a Torchbearer for his long service to the Highlands and Islands. Here he holds the Olympic Torch in front of Urquhart Castle on Loch Ness.

BELOW RIGHT: The Olympic Torch is given pride of place as it travels across Loch Ness on a RIB en route from Fort Augustus, via Dumnadrochit, to the RockNess Festival. Torchbearer Blair Marquis' most recent role has been in planning to make the musical festival a safe and successful event.

FAR RIGHT: RockNess Festival director Jim King displays the Olympic Torch after he surprised rock revellers by receiving the Flame on stage and lighting the Celebration Cauldron to celebrate the end of Day 22.

OPPOSITE: Tracy Moseley, a downhill mountain bike racer, gazes at the Olympic Flame from the slope of Ben Nevis on the same weekend she won her 11th World Cup race. 'Once the Torch is lit, it only burns for approximately 8 minutes, but for those 8 minutes I held the Olympic Flame very proudly … It was an amazing moment in a great location.'

ABOVE: Where eagles dare. An intrepid Davie Austin helps the Olympic Flame scale new heights on a ski-lift gondola near Ben Nevis, the highest mountain in the British Isles.

OPPOSITE: On board The Glenlee at The Tall Ship Museum in Glasgow, Torchbearer Emma Baird, 16, stands with Olympian Hamish Hardie MBE, who competed as a yachtsman in the 1948 London Olympic Games.

ABOVE RIGHT: The famous John O'Groats signpost is prepared in anticipation of the arrival of the Olympic Flame after its sojourn in the Scottish Isles of Orkney and Shetland.

RIGHT: Tara Laing, from Inverness, teaches English as a foreign language. She was nominated as a Torchbearer for her charity work in Nepal and her passion for helping give women the skills needed to pull themselves out of poverty.

111

Moment to Shine

Morna Brown,
18, from Stromness, shouted 'woo hoo' and laughed all the way as she took the Flame through Kirkwall. She was part of the team which broke the Orkney record for women's relay swimming at the 2011 Isle of Wight Island Games – a bi-annual event contested by 25 islands from around the world. Morna, who represents her local authority as a Youth Legacy Ambassador for 2014, also works for Scotland's Active Schools to promote sport for kids and is hoping to go to Africa to do voluntary work on leaving school herself.

ABOVE LEFT: Matthew Cox, manager of the most northerly swimming centre in the British Isles, carries the Olympic Torch through a Viking Guard of Honour. The route is lined by whooping and warmly dressed locals in Lerwick.

LEFT: Safe hands. Swimming coach, lifeguard and retained fireman, Torchbearer Matthew Cox takes the Flame onto a yoal, or Norwegian longboat, in a nod to part of the Shetland heritage.

OPPOSITE RIGHT: Inga Kemp, 22, stands in front of the magnificent sandstone St Magnus Cathedral, in Kirkwall, Orkney, also known as the 'Light in the North'. The cathedral was founded in 1137 by the Viking, Earl Rognvald, in honour of his uncle St Magnus.

OPPOSITE FAR RIGHT: Have Flame, will travel. The Olympic Flame is kept air-safe in a Lantern and secured in a special cradle as it is transported back by plane from its leg around the Shetland Islands.

'I just love how the Olympic Flame gets its own seat!'

A Twitter user reflects widespread delight at the Flame's status as a regular air passenger

Sacred Flame amid sacred stones. Kirsty Wade, 49, the middle distance runner who competed at the Seoul 1988 and Barcelona 1992 Games, raises the Torch at the central stone circle at Callanish on the Isle of Lewis as the sun rises at 4.20am.

'In Stornoway they're hanging out of the windows, standing on walls, as well as lining the streets. I've just spotted the pilot of the Flame plane also joining in!'

Laura Bicker, BBC Scotland

ABOVE: Katherine Milne holds aloft the Olympic Torch in Carrbridge. The gateway village to the Cairngorms National Park is named after a 1717 packhorse bridge, the oldest stone bridge in the Highlands.

OPPOSITE: Support trucks stoke anticipation on the streets as excited crowds await the arrival of the Torch Relay in the Granite City of Aberdeen.

ABOVE RIGHT: 'Roaring pride. John Mitchell, European quad bike champion, introduces the Flame to a new mode of transport as he rides out of Lewis Castle College in Stornoway.

RIGHT: Janet Mcnaughton of Uig, Lewis, said she was proud to be representing Stornoway Swimming Club where she gives lessons: 'I was delighted to see my pupils along the route. It's been a brilliant day.'

ABOVE: Flying the flag. Two spectators are thrilled to unfurl a giant Union flag in the streets of Brechin during Day 25 of the Torch Relay.

LEFT: The coastal resort of Montrose is regarded as the culture and sculpture capital of Angus with more than 20 statues dotting the town centre. Here the Olympic Flame is brought close to the statue of Joseph Hume, a doctor and Radical MP born in Montrose.

'The Olympic Flame is coming to Dundee today. My 5-year-old got up before 7am with her teddy packed to go see! It's not here until after 6pm...'

Shona Whitelaw

Moment to Shine

Andy Coogan, 95, was cheered on by thousands as he carried the Olympic Torch through Dundee on a specially adapted walking frame. Andy, from Carnoustie, Angus, was nominated by his Olympic champion great nephew Sir Chris Hoy, who claims him as his inspiration. 'Andy is a true legend,' said a tearful Hoy, recalling how his great uncle, one of Britain's best amateur athletes when the Second World War broke out, spent over three years in a Japanese prisoner of war camp in Malaya, during which he was tortured and starved, coming close to death. His dream of competing in the 1948 Olympic Games was shattered, but he battled back to fitness, founded the Tayside Amateur Athletic Club and competed in veteran athletics. 'I never thought I'd get to carry the Olympic Torch. Before the war I had hoped I might get there one day as an athlete. This is the next best thing.'

LEFT: United in Dundee. Jill Roche – a doctor, former gymnast, volleyball star and charity worker – passes the Olympic Flame to Kian Steel, aged 12, who is a promising schoolboy swimming and athletics competitor.

BELOW: 'The next best thing'. Andy Coogan, the 95-year-old great uncle of Team GB Olympic Cycling hero Sir Chris Hoy, embraces his long-awaited Olympic moment taking the Torch through Dundee.

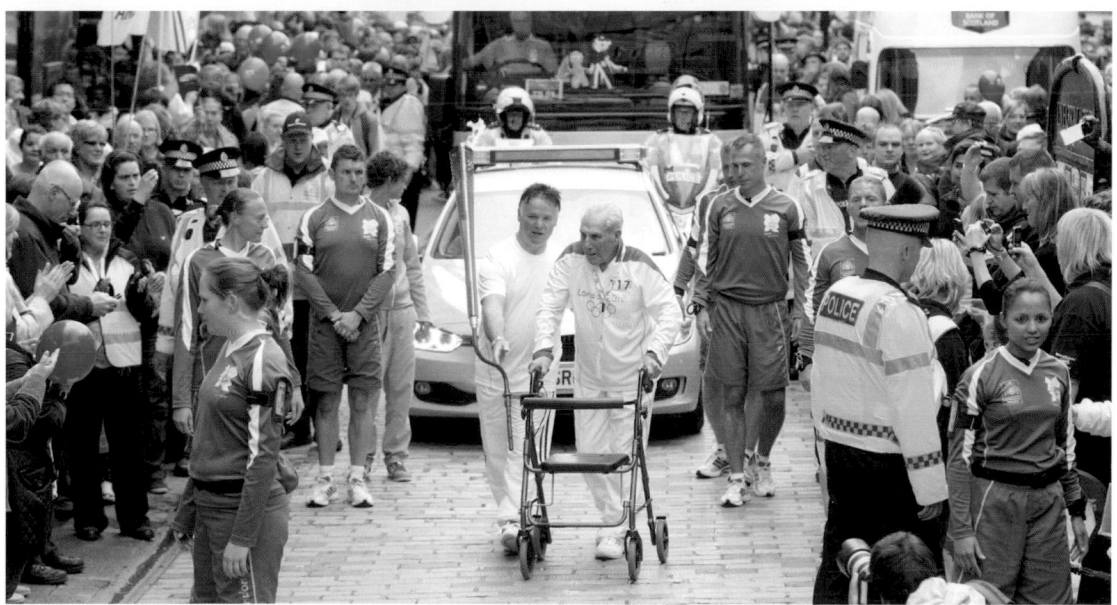

'Chariots of Fire' on West Sands Beach

Since 1981 the theme tune of the film 'Chariots of Fire' has been synonymous with British Olympic dreams. On Day 26 the Torch Relay re-created the iconic beach-run training scene for a new generation. Joseph Forrester, aged 13, carried the Torch on to West Sands Beach in St Andrews, used to portray Broadstairs in Kent for one of the film's most famous scenes, and led a group of fellow pupils at Madras College in a run along the sands. The original film, based on the true story of athletes Harold Abrahams, a Jew, and Edinburgh-born Eric Liddell, a devout Christian, at the 1924 Paris Olympic Games, was re-released in cinemas to celebrate London 2012.

Back to the Paris 1924 Games. Joseph Forrester, aged 13, leads a pack of fellow school runners from Madras College along West Sands Beach in St Andrews in a re-enactment of the opening scene of 'Chariots of Fire'.

'I'm on top of the world – I'm holding back the tears.'

Children's sports coach Sophie Hanson, 29, describes carrying the Olympic Torch

LEFT: John Wasyl Beaton-Hawryluk, 19, from South Queensferry, overcame early struggles because of dyspraxia and Asperger's diagnoses to referee rugby, lead scouts and become a member of the youth parliament. He carries the Olympic Torch on to the steps of Hopetoun House en route to Edinburgh.

ABOVE: 'How 'bout that?' The American philanthropist John Stephens, also known by his singer-songwriter stage name of John Legend, carries the Olympic Torch with pride between Broxburn and Edinburgh on Day 26.

'It was a pleasure coming to work today! It's not every day the Olympic Torch passes my office.'

Pamela Hamilton, Kinross

ABOVE: Flagging up the Games. Spectators wave Union flags as they cheer the Torch Relay convoy between Falkirk and Skinflats.

RIGHT: Lesley Forrest, who carries the Olympic Torch up the Royal Mile in her home town of Edinburgh, competes for Scotland in the British Transplant Games after receiving a kidney in 1996. She was nominated for raising awareness of the need for organ donors.

Falkirk Wheel

The Olympic Flame's remarkable journey came to a peak as, hailed by fireworks and a chorus of vuvuzelas, it rose up on a boat at the Falkirk Wheel – a rotating boat lift which opened in 2002. The Wheel is used to connect the Forth and Clyde Canal with the Union Canal, once connected by a series of 11 locks which had fallen into disuse by the 1930s. Delighted crowds on the streets of Falkirk included children in home-made fancy dress costumes and residents waving Lion Rampant flags and Saltires as well as Union Flags.

LEFT: The Olympic Flame enjoys a whirl on a boat at the Falkirk Wheel, a rotating boat lift which opened in 2002, in the hands of Torchbearer Dennis May. Fireworks were let off to celebrate another intriguing mode of transport.

BELOW: The Team GB Men's Volleyball team pose with the Olympic Flame and the British team mascot, Pride the Lion, in front of Edinburgh Castle at the end of Day 26 of the Torch Relay.

'The Olympic Torch passes through my home county Northumberland today. Makes me feel very proud to be a Northumbrian.'

Olympic bronze medallist rower Matthew Wells, who grew up in Hexham

OPPOSITE: 'Muggle' magic. Lewis Denny, a young performer and charity fundraiser, carries the Olympic Torch through the grounds of Alnwick Castle, famously Hogwarts in the Harry Potter films.

ABOVE: Truly inspirational ladies. Claire Tattersall, who was on track to play Hockey at the Olympic Games until a cancer diagnosis 15 years ago, passes the Olympic Flame to Sally Hyder, an MS sufferer and mountaineer who raises funds for Canine Partners.

RIGHT: Come rain or shine, large crowds welcomed the Torch Relay on its journey through Scotland and the Borders. The excitement of watching 'living history' captured the imagination of all ages.

Moment to Shine

Arthur Basstoe, 81, is an inspiration to his family and community in Berwick-upon-Tweed. During last winter he hiked daily to the nearest shop three miles away with his rucksack, through 1m of snow, to help his elderly neighbour; he also cleared driveways and paths eight times for neighbours. He looks after his wife who is a wheelchair user, despite having prostate cancer himself. His motto for life is: 'If you stop, you'll never get started again!' Brought up in the East End of London, Arthur used to run in 800m races as a member of his local athletics club, Eton Manor – now the site of the Olympic Stadium.

ABOVE LEFT: Emma Pringle, 20, a dedicated triple jumper, covered three legs of the Torch Relay through her home town of Alnwick – from Alnwick Garden's entrance on Denwick Lane, through the iconic Hotspur Tower and up to Clayport Street.

LEFT: Attention! The second battalion of the Royal Highland Fusiliers prepare to cheer Torchbearer Philip Craze minutes before the Torch Relay convoy passes through Milton Bridge.

'Lovely atmosphere on my Metro packed with schoolchildren in waterproofs and GB flags on the way to Whitley Bay for the Torch Relay.'

Tweeted by Simon Roffe

LEFT: Sam Smith, whose goal-scoring exploits at powerchair football are inspirational to all, receives the Flame for his Torch Relay leg. His motto is: 'you don't have to be an elite athlete to make an impact.'

BELOW: Inner sanctum. Tony Holland brandishes the Torch inside the gate of Warkworth Castle. One of the largest and most impressive medieval fortresses in north east England, it was once home to the Percy family.

'It's a fantastic vibe despite the weather. The atmosphere is incredible.'

Fab Flournoy from the Newcastle Eagles basketball team in Blyth

ABOVE: The Torch Relay Security Team use a mobile windbreak to keep the Flame alight in rain and blustery conditions.

LEFT: Chief Scout and TV adventurer Bear Grylls slides down a 400m zipwire to take the Olympic Flame across the River Tyne. 'I was kind of worried about the Flame going out, but it stayed alight – it was amazing,' he said after landing safely in the parade ground of HMS Calliope.

OPPOSITE: Hoods up, wellies on, balloons and flags at the ready. Excited schoolchildren wait to glimpse the Olympic Flame by the roadside in Bedlington.

OVERLEAF: Tyne Bridge at night. The city of Newcastle, famous for its sporting passion, celebrates the Olympic Torch Relay with a display of the Olympic rings on its landmark bridge.

Week 4 Places

SATURDAY Glasgow • Bearsden • Clydebank • Dumbarton • Luss • Tarbet • Crianlarich • Tyndrum • Glencoe • North Ballachullish • Fort William • Spean Bridge • Fort Augustus • Invermoriston • Lewiston • Drumnadrochit • Inverness **SUNDAY** Kirkwall (Orkney Islands) • Lerwick (Shetland Islands) **MONDAY** Stornoway • Inverness • Aviemore • Carrbridge • Grantown-on-Spey • Tomintoul • Crathie • Ballater • Dinnet • Aboyne • Kincardine O'Neil • Banchory • Drumoak • Peterculter • Bieldside • Cults • Aberdeen **TUESDAY** Aberdeen • Stonehaven • Marykirk • Hillside • Montrose • Brechin • Forfar • Meigle • Coupar Angus • Woodside • Burrelton • Balbeggie • Scone • Scone Palace • Perth • Abernethy • Newburgh • Cupar • Dairsie • Guardbridge • Leuchars • Dundee

WEDNESDAY St. Andrews • Milnathort • Kinross • Crook of Devon • Alloa • Bridge of Allan • Dunblane • Stirling • Cumbernauld • Larbert • Camelon • Falkirk • Skinflats • Cairneyhill • Crossford • Dunfermline • Hopetoun House • Broxburn • Edinburgh **THURSDAY** Edinburgh • Duddingston • Musselburgh • Dalkeith • Lasswade • Loanhead • Bilston • Milton Bridge • Penicuik • Eddleston • Peebles • Innerleithen • Walkerburn • Selkirk • Galashiels • Earlston • Gordon • Greenlaw • Duns • Chirnside • Foulden • Berwick-Upon-Tweed • Bamburgh • Alnwick **FRIDAY** Alnwick • Hipsburn • Warkworth • Amble • Ashington • Newbiggin-By-The-Sea • Ashington • Choppington • Morpeth • Hartford • Bedlington • Blyth • Whitley Bay • Cullercoats • Tynemouth • North Shields • Howdon • Wallsend • Newcastle upon Tyne

Chapter 5
16 to 22 June

Highlights

What a spectacular start to Day 29. The Flame abseiled down the mirrored windows of The Sage in Gateshead and by nighttime was displayed in its Celebration Cauldron after a rainbow appeared above Durham's Castle and Cathedral. In between came a celebration of athletics as legendary Ethiopian Haile Gebrselassie 'kissed' Torches with Brendan Foster and Steve Cram 'walked on water' (booms over water) at the Sunderland Aquatic Centre. Other highlights included an attempt at the world hula-hooping record at Herrington Country Park, a visit to Hadrian's Wall and the Flame passing under Antony Gormley's iconic Angel of the North sculpture.

England and Durham cricketer Paul Collingwood fielded the Torch outside Durham Cathedral as crowds waved it off – its destination Middlesbrough. Father's Day brought out lots of children on their fathers' shoulders. Locals on the routes marked the occasion in idiosyncratic ways – enjoying mid-morning beers in Blackhall Colliery, ringing bells from towers in Hartlepool and scrambling up lamp posts in Billingham.

Congratulations to Torchbearer David State and to Christine Langham, who accepted his public marriage proposal (phew!) midway through his Torch Relay slot on Day 31. Prior to that romantic interlude, the Flame had visited Middlesbrough's Transporter Bridge before heading off to the Victorian coastal resorts of Redcar and Saltburn. It received a pirate salute in Whitby, a lift to Pickering on board the Sir Nigel Gresley (the fastest recorded steam locomotive since the Second World War) and an ovation at Scarborough Open Air Theatre. The sun came out, the Torch Security Team's matching shades went on, and the Flame scorched along Scarborough's colourful seafront.

An aquatic theme characterised Day 32. The Flame's lustre competed with fluorescent fish inside The Deep aquarium in Hull and journeyed past Spurn Lightship and Hull's marina. In Brough everyone was out on bunting-laden streets, or in deckchairs at the end of driveways. HRH Princess Beatrice of York welcomed the party to Harewood House in Leeds. York had entertainment to satisfy all palates – from a chocolate version of the Torch to an escort of 200 cyclists, to a trip along its Roman city walls. The final Torchbearer of the day into York Racecourse was Harvey Smith on his novice show jumper Paddy.

York Minster provided the starting blocks for the journey northwest to Carlisle. Steam buffs were thrilled as the Scots Guardsman bore the Flame from York's National Railway Museum to Thirsk with a pipe and drum send-off from the First Battalion, the Scots Guard Regiment. Barnard's Castle was alive with the buzz, while Brough provided a perfect carnival warm-up for the evening celebration in Bitts Park, Carlisle.

Dumfries, known as the Queen of the South, gave the Flame a right royal welcome. Hundreds of people gathered as Kenny Loggins' 'Footloose' gave way to a pipe band playing 'Scotland the Brave'. Soon, it was farewell to Scotland… Cumbrian weather challenged the Flame, but not the mood. A sea of soggy replica 'Torches' greeted the convoy in Whitehaven. Stepladders were out in Cockermouth to help people see as the convoy passed by. Spectacular Lake District scenery mesmerised all en route to Keswick. Ambleside displayed a tree made of gold balloons. The Flame then voyaged across Lake Windermere in a steamer towards a spirited evening celebration in Bowness-on-Windermere.

Day 35 marked the Torch Relay's halfway point and saw the Flame edge down the northwest coast, from Kendal to Milnthorpe, Carnforth, Bolton-le-Sands, Morecambe and Lancaster. Battling through wind and rain, Olympic silver medallist Debbie Flood was the most aptly named Torchbearer as the Flame made its way towards Blackpool. In Morecambe the Torch was photographed in front of the statue of comedian Eric Morecambe. High winds forced the cancellation of its ascent up Blackpool Tower, but 'Strictly Come Dancing' champions Harry Judd and Aliona Vilani shimmied indoors on the famous dancefloor in a special Viennese Waltz set to Queen's 'We are the Champions'. It made a rousing end to a valiantly supported Week 5.

All white on the night. 'Strictly Come Dancing' champions, pop star Harry Judd and his dance partner Aliona Vilani, don official Torchbearer outfits to take the Olympic Torch for a spin. They performed to Queen's anthem 'We are the Champions' inside Blackpool's Tower Ballroom.

RIGHT: Richard Jackson, one of the window-cleaning team at The Sage music hall, abseils down its side in Gateshead. 'Flames and ropes don't mix so I had one eye on the Torch, one eye on the ropes, one eye on my feet and one eye on the public! I couldn't take it all in – it was an amazing feeling and I'll reflect on it later with a lot of pride,' he said.

BELOW: Iris Hutchinson poses under the 'embrace' of the Angel of the North. She was nominated for 'making a difference to lots of people by listening and caring' as a local volunteer.

Angel of the North

Large numbers of spectators followed as Torchbearer Iris Hutchinson passed under the Angel of the North. Nominated for her charity work with Marie Curie and a local soup kitchen, Iris had the honour of carrying the Flame past Antony Gormley's sculpture. Wrought from 200 tonnes of steel, giving an open-armed welcome to all visitors to Gateshead, Tyne and Wear, the sculpture stands 20m tall and has a wingspan of 54m. This is the equivalent of being as tall as four double decker buses with a wingspan as broad as that of a jumbo jet.

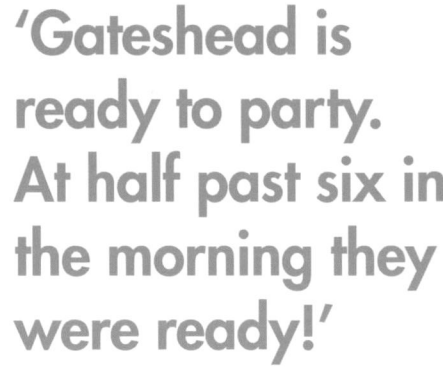

'Gateshead is ready to party. At half past six in the morning they were ready!'

Steph Kinnon

OPPOSITE: Just as she does as a disability football referee, Charlotte Proud, 20, who suffers from brittle bone disease, 'runs the line' along Hadrian's Wall with the Olympic Torch at Housesteads Roman Fort in Northumberland.

Moment to Shine

Mia Rathband, 13, the daughter of PC David Rathband who was blinded by gunman Raoul Moat in 2010, walked with the Torch through South Tyneside. Her father – much admired for setting up the Blue Lamp Foundation charity, helping emergency services personnel injured in the line of duty – had been nominated to carry the Flame. Following his death in February, Mia asked to take his place. She wore a black blindfold in recognition of what happened to her father. Mia's mother Kath said she knew David would have been 'very proud to see Mia carry the Torch on his behalf'.

ABOVE: The Flame is carried around Gateshead International Stadium by Jon Mellish, 14. His commitment to sports – football, rugby and athletics – at school and club level earned him an overall sports personality prize in the South Tyneside sports awards.

RIGHT: Mia Rathband is blindfolded in recognition of what happened to her late father. She ran with the Flame on the leg that had been assigned to PC Rathband before his death in February 2012.

'The Olympic Flame has been all over the world and to come to a small village like Whitburn is a bit special.'

Barry Emmerson

LEFT: Knocking them for six. England and Durham cricketer Paul Collingwood starts his innings with the Olympic Torch on the green outside Durham's magnificent Norman cathedral.

TOP: Best seats in the house. Young flag-wavers enjoy the vantage point from a car roof as the Olympic Flame passes through Stockton-on-Tees.

ABOVE: Imran Naeem, a Public Health Officer, greets his mother before his Torch Relay slot through Harrowgate Hill. He works endlessly across all communities on a range of sporting initiatives.

Moment to Shine

Kay Stokes, 53, ran with the Flame in Newton Aycliffe. She has been instrumental in the development of triathlon in the region, both as an active volunteer and coach. She runs the Cleveland Triathlon Club junior academy, coaching children and organising annual training camps, social outings and workshops. Kay also takes an adult coaching group and encouraged a British Triathlon Disabled squad member to take up the sport. Her enthusiasm is unyielding: she helped found a women and girls Try-a-Tri campaign in 2008 alongside the Women's Sport and Fitness Foundation. She aided the delivery of the Corus Kids of Steel initiative on Teesside, aimed at encouraging children of all backgrounds to participate in triathlon.

ABOVE: The towering structure and thundering cannons of HMS Trincomalee welcome the Flame and Torchbearer Jamie Poole, a primary school sports teacher. The oldest British warship still afloat, it was a tribute to Hartlepool's seafaring tradition.

RIGHT: Lawrence Smith, 85, a community stalwart nominated by his grandchild for 'being an inspiration to me and the rest of my family through many life crises', embraces a spectator as he carries the Olympic Torch through Blackhall Colliery.

OPPOSITE: On a platform next to steam locomotive The Green Knight, pride of the North Yorkshire Moors Railway, Kelly Williams holds up the Olympic Torch. Kelly is a passionate PE teacher whose mission is to 'bring happiness to children through sport.'

ABOVE: A view of the Middlesbrough Transporter Bridge, the starting point for Day 31. The 69m high bridge is a symbol of the area's industrial heritage and celebrates its centenary this year.

ABOVE LEFT: Bridging the gap. Janet Nolan works tirelessly as the Chair of the Special Olympics Yorkshire and Humber Committee while caring for her daughter, May, who has Down's Syndrome. Here she poses with the Olympic Torch in front of the Humber Bridge in Hull.

ABOVE: The big question. David State, a special police constable, thrills the crowds by proposing on one knee to his girlfriend Christine during his Torch Relay slot.

LEFT: Jamie Green, 25, the Children's Patron at young people's mobility charity Whizz-Kidz, takes to the stage with the Olympic Flame at Scarborough Open Air Theatre.

ABOVE: Philip Jones's stint with the Olympic Torch highlights the wonder of York's Roman city walls. The walls extend for 4km, enclose an area of 263 acres and still retain all four of their impressive gateways as well as 34 of their 39 interval towers.

LEFT: Olympic show jumper Harvey Smith carries the Torch into York Racecourse on his horse Paddy. The 74-year-old, whose two sons also competed at the Games, lit the Celebration Cauldron saying, 'I'm very honoured for the whole of Yorkshire to do this for them.'

RIGHT: Rays of light. A blue spotted ribbontail stingray looks on as Erica Hughes takes the Olympic Torch on an aquarium adventure inside The Deep in Hull.

ABOVE: Ted Haughey strides out through an enthusiastic tunnel of support in Brough. He was nominated by his wife for his sterling fundraising runs for the Children's Heart Unit Fund at the Freeman hospital, as well as for the charity De Paul UK who help homeless and disadvantaged young people.

OPPOSITE: 'Is it nearly here yet?' The magnetic attraction of the Olympic Flame brings out local schoolchildren in Barkston Ash, ready with their Union flags and stunning homemade 'Torches'.

Aysgarth Falls

Film buffs might recognise Aysgarth Falls as the site where Robin Hood and Little John fought in the Kevin Costner epic 'Robin Hood Prince of Thieves'. The Falls are a triple flight of waterfalls, carved out by the River Ure as it flows through Wensleydale in Yorkshire. They were created during the Ice Age, when heavy rivers of ice ground down the valleys. Today, the river stretches out along the valley and dramatically drops 30 metres.

ABOVE: Pretty as a postcard. Frederick Collett passes on the Olympic Flame to Caroline Curtis in front of Aysgarth Falls, a spectacular stretch of water in Lower Wensleydale, Yorkshire. Thousands of gallons of water cascade over rock ledges in a dramatic triple tier of waterfalls.

'Seeing the people of Penrith getting behind the Torch Relay and the Olympic Games, the enthusiasm, warmth and breadth of people ... was a very moving and special experience.'

Sir Chris Bonington, who lives in Penrith

ABOVE RIGHT: Surgeon Eugene Perry – pictured here at Sutton Bank, in the North York Moors National Park, with the Vale of York in the background – was nominated for his heavy involvement in local football and cricket activities.

RIGHT: Pomp and circumstance. Members of the First Battalion, the Scots Guards wait beside the Scots Guardsman steam locomotive before giving the Olympic Flame a traditional pipe-and-drum send-off.

LEFT: Helen Jackson, who works in local hospices caring for terminally ill people, has her moment to shine at the Norman Richmond Castle. Its magnificent views overlook the Yorkshire Dales.

BELOW: Local hero Bob Sutcliffe, who runs a swimming school with his wife Jan and recently became a junior school teacher, proudly takes the Flame through Appleby-in-Westmorland.

Moment to Shine

Terry Deary, whose *Horrible History* books have turned a generation of children into history lovers, surprised children at Parkside Sports College, Durham with the revelation he always hated history at school because it was taught in such a boring way. Terry runs regularly for many charities, has completed the 10km run at Sunderland Tyne & Wear and aims to motivate young people to do exercise and join him on various fun runs in the area. He is an inspiration to everyone he meets.

145

ABOVE: A patriotic pit stop. Local residents display their red, white and blue on umbrellas, flags and a vintage car to celebrate a moment of history as the Torch Relay passes through Keswick.

ABOVE RIGHT: Rosemary McFarlane, who raises funds to bring heart screening to Fife and Edinburgh following the sudden loss of her young husband Greg, passes the Olympic Flame to Andrew Brodie of the Cumbria Fire and Rescue Service in Keswick.

RIGHT: Carry on burning. The Cumbrian weather challenged the Flame, but never the mood of the communities it travelled through en route south to Blackpool.

'The crowds are out in Wigton and there's an instant festival atmosphere. The Flame is burning brightly against the grey sky.'

Jennie Dennett

BOTTOM LEFT: Rain fails to dampen the enthusiasm of the crowds lining the streets and taking up their positions to welcome the Olympic Flame to their home town.

BELOW: Schoolchildren wrap up against the wind and the rain as they happily enjoy a morning out of the classroom to witness history in the making.

FAR LEFT: Safely housed in a Lantern, the Olympic Flame is protected from the elements as the Torch Relay goes into convoy mode.

LEFT: The Olympic Flame takes to the waters of Lake Windermere on board historic steam boat The Tern, accompanied by teenage Torchbearer Stephanie Booth and groups of local schoolchildren.

OPPOSITE: Dancing in the dark. The Olympic Torch is held aloft in the ruins of 12th-century Kendal Castle. This popular walking spot affords fantastic views over the town and surrounding countryside.

'Liz Auld brought a tear to my eye – how lovely it was for her to allow everyone a good look at the Torch.'

Julie Cutler Worthington

A Welcome at Lake Windermere

On Day 34 of the Torch Relay, the Flame was transported across Lake Windermere, the largest natural lake in England, on steamboat The Tern. A flotilla accompanied the Flame and Torchbearer Stephanie Booth across the lake that has hosted the Great North Swim since 2008. Stephanie, 14, a talented triathlete from Windermere, noted with relief at the end of her Torchbearer duties, 'I was very nervous at the start because I didn't want to singe anyone's hair and everyone kept coming up to me. It would have been a bit embarrassing.'

RIGHT: Former Scots Guardsman David Watson, who lost three limbs while on patrol in Afghanistan in 2010, carries the Torch through Lancaster accompanied by pipers from his old regiment.

BELOW: All aboard! Peter Cunningham, a pastor who works with the homeless and young people, introduces the Olympic Flame to Britain's first electric tramway, travelling to West Drive in Blackpool.

BELOW RIGHT: Gale-force fun. Umbrellas are turned inside out by the wind as spectators cheer the Flame in Lancaster.

'Absolutely soaked, freezing and covered in mud, but seeing the Flame has been fun!'

Katy Atkinson

LEFT: Shelly Woods, a Paralympic athlete whose specialities are 1500m, 5000m and the marathon, carries the Olympic Torch through her home town of Blackpool. She brought home a silver and a bronze medal from the Beijing 2008 Games.

ABOVE: Bring me sunshine. Victoria Brier holds the Olympic Torch in front of the statue of much-loved comedian Eric Morecambe, in his classic 'skip dance' pose, in Morecambe.

OVERLEAF: Underneath the arches. Lewis Birkinshaw, 17, takes the Olympic Torch through the church interior of Fountains Abbey near Ripon in Yorkshire. Lewis was nominated for being 'a learner who is highly successful in both academic and sporting worlds'.

Week 5 Places

SATURDAY Gateshead • South Shields • Whitburn • Sunderland • Low Fell & Chowdene • Blaydon • Prudhoe • Stocksfield • Hexham • Riding Mill • Consett • Moorside • Castleside • Tow Law • Esh • Langley Park • Durham

SUNDAY Durham • Sherburn • Sherburn Hill • Haswell Plough • Peterlee • Horden • Blackhall Colliery • Hartlepool • Billingham • Sedgefield • Bishop Auckland • Shildon • Middridge • Newton Aycliffe • High Beaumont Hill • Harrowgate Hill • Darlington • Stockton-on-Tees • Middlesbrough **MONDAY** Middlesbrough • Redcar • Marske-by-the-Sea • Saltburn-by-the-Sea • Brotton • Carlin How • Loftus • Hinderwell • Lythe • Sandsend • Whitby • Pickering • Scarborough • Filey • Bridlington • Beverley • Hull **TUESDAY** Hull • Brough • Goole • Camblesforth • Selby • Monk Fryston • Barkston Ash • Tadcaster • Boston Spa • Wetherby • Harewood • Knaresborough • Harrogate • Ripon • York **WEDNESDAY** York • Thirsk • Northallerton • Aiskew • Bedale • Aysgarth • Leyburn • Richmond • Barnard Castle • Brough • Appleby-in-Westmorland • Penrith • Carlisle **THURSDAY** Dumfries in Galloway • Annan • Eastriggs • Gretna • Carlisle • Wigton • Aspatria • Maryport • Flimby • Workington • Whitehaven • Cockermouth • Keswick • Grasmere • Ambleside • Bowness-on-Windermere **FRIDAY** Kendal • Milnthorpe • Carnforth • Bolton-le-Sands • Hest Bank • Morecambe • Lancaster • Garstang • St Michael's On Wyre • Fleetwood • Cleveleys • Blackpool

Chapter 6
23 to 29 June

Highlights

Week 6 of the Torch Relay teed off at Royal Lytham & St Annes Golf Club. Storms had struck in the night, but there wasn't a spare inch of pavement along the route. The sight of a father and son riding on a tandem to keep up with the convoy was a lovely cameo. Blackburn greeted the Flame with a choir and a relieved MP. 'I thought "cripes" in the night with the howling gale,' said Jack Straw. Anyone who stayed indoors hung out of windows. Gurinder Chadha, director of the film 'Bend it Like Beckham', carried the Flame – straight – in Burnley. Sports-mad Manchester was thronged with people poised to party in Albert Square.

The next day the Flame set off behind the handlebars of BMX racer Shanaze Reade from Media City in Salford en route to Leeds. Sir Bobby Charlton, the former Manchester United star and a member of England's 1966 World Cup-winning side, carried the Flame up Sir Matt Busby Way to Old Trafford. A 'Tameside's Got Talent' Olympic plinth in Ashton-under-Lyne invited those inspired by the Torch Relay to perform in five-minute slots. Oldham celebrated with Games-themed family activities while Brighouse

held a mini Olympic Games. Colin Moynihan, Olympic rowing cox and chairman of the British Olympic Association, enjoyed a slot as a Torchbearer. The Flame visited Bradford's Centenary Square and the world famous Headingley cricket ground before attending an evening picnic at the historic estate of Temple Newsam in Leeds.

And so on to Sheffield via Barnsley, with a Yorkshire reception full of northern warmth and hospitality. As Phil Bodmer of BBC Look North commented, 'I can't recall in my 20-odd years of broadcasting so many people coming together.' Sebastian Coe, Chair of LOCOG and a double gold (1500m) and silver (800m) medallist in the 1980 Moscow and 1984 Los Angeles Games, proudly took the Flame for a 'bouncy and jolly' run through his home city of Sheffield.

The Olympic Flame's impact on local communities is in evidence every day, but on Day 39 – when the Torch Relay left Sheffield, city of steel, for Cleethorpes on the Lincolnshire coast – the image of one special Torchbearer aroused national admiration. Ben Parkinson, severely injured by an anti-tank mine in Afghanistan in 2006 and not expected to survive, completed an epic Torch Relay stint to loud applause. Earlier in the day, the Flame had dazzled against fiery backdrops as it made its way through the MAGNA Science Adventure Centre in the hands of poet and storyteller Debjani Chatterjee.

Day 40 brought a daredevil start as the Flame abseiled down Grimsby's Royal Dock Tower. Lincolnshire is famous for

RIGHT: Don't look down. Alan Ellinson kicks off Day 40 of the Torch Relay by abseiling down the 94m high Royal Dock Tower in Grimsby. Together with his partner and son, Alan opened the Rope Race Climbing Centre in 1993 to allow people of all ages and abilities to take part in the sport.

its sausages, and in Louth the Torch Relay was greeted by the mayoress dressed up as a 2.5m tall chipolata. In Mumby, decibel levels rocketed courtesy of five coachloads of schoolchildren. The Flame took a turn around the Skegness Clock Tower, visited historic Sleaford and crossed agricultural fenland to arrive in the cathedral city of Lincoln. The city was festooned with flags, balloons and streamers, while overhead at the Evening Celebration the ever brilliant Red Arrows created sky-bunting with smoke trails in red, white and blue.

Thunder, lightning and rain struck the Torch Relay on the day it touched imaginations with a visit to Sherwood Forest, home of Robin Hood and Maid Marian. Later in the day, in a specially choreographed Bolero, the Torch was twirled around by Olympic gold medalists, Jayne Torvill and Christopher Dean on the ice rink in Nottingham where they trained. Week 6 ended with more torrential rain, and even more cheery nonchalance about the weather. The Flame visited Newstead Abbey, once the home of Lord Byron, and Chatsworth, seat of the Duke of Devonshire; it also rode a cable car to scale The Heights of Abraham in the Peak District and met the former World Superbike champion James Toseland, who lit the Celebration Cauldron in Derby.

ABOVE: Two boys relax in the five interlocking Olympic rings. Designed in 1912 by Baron Pierre de Coubertin, the rings represent the union of the five continents and the meeting of athletes from all nations at the Olympic Games.

RIGHT: Flag waving in the rain. On the route between Bury and Rawtenstall in Lancashire, patriotic spectators in Union flag raincoats cheer on the Olympic Flame.

Moment to Shine

Ryan Thornton, 25, was 19 when his older brother Lee was killed in Iraq. Gunner Lee Thornton, aged 22, was serving with the Royal Artillery when he was shot by a sniper while out on patrol, a devastating loss for the whole family. Ryan became one of the founding members of the Soldiers, Sailors, Airmen and Families Association Help Support Group for bereaved siblings. He has worked hard over the last two years to make sure that anyone who has lost a sibling in service knows about the group. 'When my brother died in Iraq I didn't speak to anyone about it. But this group helped me build my confidence. We meet up and talk about what we have been through,' he says. Now 25, Ryan chairs the meetings and welcomes new members to make sure they feel part of the group. He also works with children with disabilities and additional support needs.

OPPOSITE: Leehom Wang, 36, from Taipei City jumps for joy as he performs with the Olympic Flame through Manchester. The American-born singer-songwriter was also a Torchbearer at Beijing 2008 and performed in the Closing Ceremony at the time.

ABOVE: Wedding rings. The Olympic rings are emblazoned on the front of St James The Less Roman Catholic church in Rawtenstall, as newlyweds Catherine Lloyd and Darren Heys welcome the Flame to their celebrations.

LEFT: A fanfare from Wardle High Youth Band accompanies the Torch 'kiss' of Wensheng Li and Amy Peckover by Rochdale Town Hall. During her slot, Amy was followed by eight Rochdale Olympic cars.

Moment to Shine

Robert Littlewood, 44, who ran in Oldham, helps young people living in supported housing. He recently secured enough money to open a mixed martial arts gym in Ashton-under-Lyne and has been working for crime reduction charity NACRO for six years. 'I've worked hard to keep people out of jail through sport, and it is very humbling to have this honour by way of recognising my work. It's a special day, and provides me with an opportunity to inspire more kids who might be going down the wrong path in life.'

OPPOSITE: Former middle distance runner Diane Modahl competed in four Olympic Games: Seoul 1988, Barcelona 1992, Atlanta 1996 and Sydney 2000. Here the mother of three and ambassador for StreetGames, a charity for inner-city children, takes the Flame through Preston.

ABOVE RIGHT: Hundreds of people brave the rain and the early start to witness Sir Bobby Charlton take the Olympic Flame past Old Trafford football stadium. A member of the 1966 World Cup winning team, he said of the experience, 'This is magic. This is a great place and the fans have been amazing'.

RIGHT: Excited spectators use every vantage point as the Olympic Flame passes between Ashton-under-Lyne and Oldham.

LEFT: A golden moment. Aaron Bell, 13, carries the Torch into the historic estate of Temple Newsam in Leeds on Day 37. A black belt in karate, Aaron is a role model to younger children in training, and hopes to be British champion one day.

BELOW: Team GB's BMX world champion Shanaze Reade rides the Torch through a colourful blizzard of confetti in Salford Quays. Having already competed at Beijing 2008, Shanaze was selected for London 2012 in June, and is a major medal hope.

LEFT: Front gardens in Batley fill with spectators keen to celebrate the moment when the drama of the Olympic Games passes their own front door.

BELOW LEFT: Going underground. Museum guides Stephen Oxley (left) and Bob White (right) proudly display the Olympic Flame in its Lantern – modelled on the traditional Davy lamp, created in 1815 for use in coal mines to reduce the danger of explosions – at the National Coal Mining Museum in Wakefield.

BELOW: Local schoolchildren in Dewsbury wave homemade 'Torches' and shake plastic hand clappers, as they watch the convoy on Day 38.

163

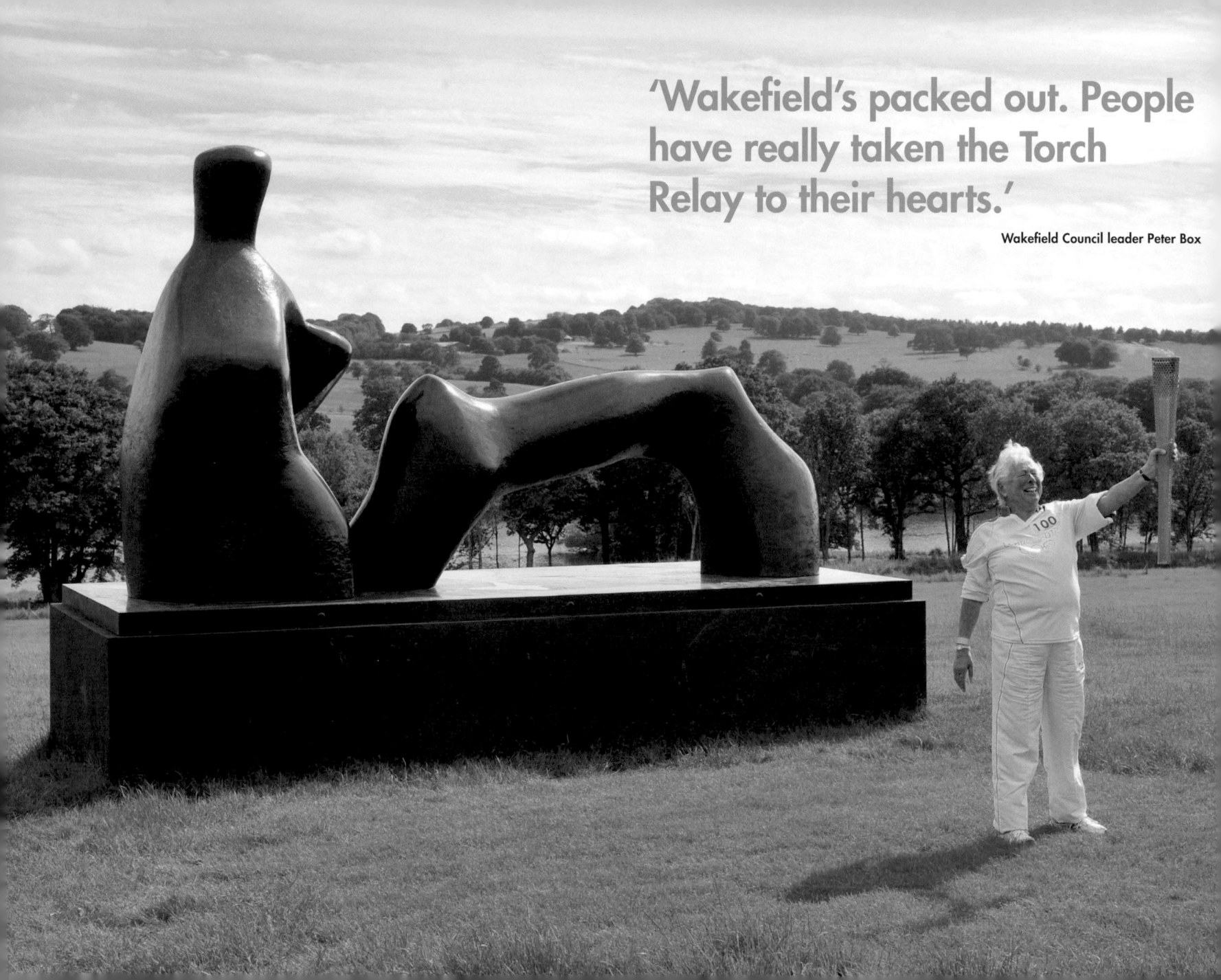

'Wakefield's packed out. People have really taken the Torch Relay to their hearts.'

Wakefield Council leader Peter Box

Jack Mitchell, 19, is from Barnsley. In January 2010 he suffered a severe traumatic brain injury and underwent 14 months in rehabilitation following life-saving surgery. With therapy and physio he has learned to eat and talk again. 'You should have heard the round of applause when he tried to walk unaided with the Torch. It was absolutely magnificent. It was one of the most emotional moments in this entire journey,' said an onlooker.

ABOVE: Lady with the Lamp. Debjani Chatterjee shows the Flame to patients at the Sheffield Children's Hospital, before running with the Torch the following day. Together with Seb Coe and Deputy Prime Minister Nick Clegg, she told the children about the history of the Olympic Flame.

OPPOSITE: Muriel Brown, 81, has given more than 60 years of inspirational service to Amateur Athletics. She carries the Torch in the Yorkshire Sculpture Park, described as 'the finest exhibition site for sculpture in the world'.

LEFT: Seb Coe, Chair of LOCOG and three-time Olympic Games medallist, carries the Flame through his home town of Sheffield. Coe said it was an honour to be a Torchbearer and there was 'nowhere else I'd rather be'.

LEFT: Letting off steam. The Flame and Torchbearer Michael Clorley hitch a lift on the Cleethorpes Coast Light Railway during Day 39. Michael, lynchpin of the Phoenix Cricket Club in Grimsby, is much admired for his indomitable spirit in battling bowel cancer, and his work to raise awareness of the disease.

BELOW: Lucy Brunt, aged 13, completes a lap at the Don Valley Stadium in Sheffield, in front of large crowds of supporters. Lucy, known to her sports coaches as 'The Little Star', was nominated for her work with the disability sport project Within Reach.

BELOW: Eat your heart out, Usain Bolt! Ben Pacey (left), a former British water polo team member who lost two years of training because of a leukaemia diagnosis, re-enacts the sprinter's famous victory salute as he exchanges the Flame with Archie Swain in Scunthorpe.

RIGHT: Debjani Chatterjee sparks imaginations as she holds the Olympic Torch next to The Big Melt at the MAGNA Science Adventure Centre in Yorkshire. An inspiring, Indian-born poet, writer and storyteller, Debjani is the author of more than 50 books.

Moment to Shine

Ben Parkinson

joined the Paratroopers at the age of 17 and was serving in Iraq by 18. While on deployment in Afghanistan in 2006, he was injured by an anti-tank mine. Losing both legs and suffering a massive brain injury, he was not expected to survive. Defying all odds, he made it through and now has prosthetic limbs and has learned to speak again. He spends his time raising money for military charities. Ben was determined to walk his 300m stretch through Doncaster. It took him 30 minutes. Walking behind him, members of his former regiment, dressed in military fatigues and red berets urged him on every step of the way, clapping and shouting 'Go Ben'.

Major David Walker, Ben's commanding officer, said, 'I'm just about managing to keep it together. Ben's tenacity and sheer courage and determination is amazing.'

'I'm in tears watching this wonderful man. I'll never ever forget those images. Very proud of Doncaster's support too.'

Lisa Brunton Stocks

LEFT: Huge crowds cheer war veteran Ben Parkinson as he carries the Torch through Doncaster with members of his former regiment in battle fatigues. He spends 12 hours a day in the gym and rehabilitation, spending the rest of his time fundraising for military charities.

OPPOSITE: Donkeys watch with approval as Starr Halley holds the Olympic Torch on Skegness Beach. 'It was epic, just amazing,' said the 15-year-old, who is overcoming a brain tumour and is active in charity work.

ABOVE: Nicholas Hope takes emotional leave of his son as he begins his Torch Relay slot through Lincoln. A passionate volunteer who strongly believes in improving the lives of young people in his neighbourhood, his son's sign read, 'Well Done Dad, We're Really Proud of You!'

RIGHT: What a turnout! Torchbearer Starr Halley waves to the crowd as she is overwhelmed by the support on Skegness Beach. She later noted, 'I was so nervous, but once you've got it in your hand … you've just got to do it.'

The Royal Dock Tower, Grimsby

Alan Ellinson, 55, has helped charities raise more than £12m through abseiling and zip wire events. On Day 40, Alan abseiled down The Royal Dock Tower in Grimsby with the Torch. Grimsby, a gateway to the North Sea, was in the early 1900s one of the world's premier fishing ports. The Royal Dock Tower is a symbol of the town's importance as a port and was officially opened by Queen Victoria and Prince Albert in 1854. The tower is 94 metres tall and was designed by James William Wild in the style of Palazzo Pubblico in Siena, Italy. The tower's purpose was to store water to provide hydraulic pressure to operate lock gates and supply drinking water to ships, the fish market and houses on the dock estate.

ABOVE LEFT: Sky bunting. A flypast of Red Arrows streams red, white and blue vapour trails at the Yarborough Sports Ground. The Red Arrows team, based at RAF Scampton in Lincolnshire, will perform at the London 2012 Opening Ceremony.

LEFT: On the brink. Torchbearer Alan Ellinson begins his 94m abseil down The Royal Dock Tower in Grimsby. His safe descent took place a month to the day to the Opening Ceremony of the London 2012 Games.

LEFT: An early start didn't dampen the enthusiasm of these excited schoolchildren waiting for the arrival of Dorothy Fraser, the first Torchbearer of Day 41, at Lincoln Cathedral.

BELOW LEFT: Perfect 10! Jayne Torvill and Christopher Dean, gold medallists at the 1984 Winter Olympic Games, replicate their ice dance perfection with the lit Torch in Nottingham Ice Arena – where their own dream began.

Torvill and Dean

Jayne Torvill and Christopher Dean became household names when they won gold with perfect scores at the 1984 Winter Olympic Games in Sarajevo. The ice-dance pair from Nottingham performed a specially choreographed routine with the lit Torch in hand at Nottingham Ice Arena, later lighting the Celebration Cauldron at the city's evening celebration. 'It was amazing to think we could be here in Nottingham, where all our Olympic dreams started. The Torch Relay represents the spirit of the Olympic Games, and it's a rallying cry for the whole nation to get behind,' said Dean. 'Winning Olympic gold was a great moment, but this is right up there,' added Torvill.

Trees frame Torchbearer Laura Graves as she carries the Torch through Sherwood Forest. In the area made famous by the Robin Hood legend, Laura was greeted by a 21st-century Robin Hood before she began her slot.

'The Torch Relay finally comes to Nottingham today and the heavens are working hard to extinguish it! Better get my wellies.'

Gaynor Drake

173

LEFT: Fur and feathers. A spectator brings his pet Barn Owl and West Highland Terrier to enjoy the Torch Relay celebrations as the convoy passes through Nottingham.

ABOVE: Excited family crowds enjoy their good vantage point as they wait for their bird's-eye glimpse of the Olympic Flame on the road between Calow and Chesterfield in Derbyshire.

OPPOSITE: Chatsworth, owned by the Duke and Duchess of Devonshire, provides a magnificent backdrop for Olympic Torchbearer Benjamin Hope. Sixteen generations of the Cavendish family have occupied the house, surrounded by parkland, shaping the evolution of its architecture and and interior design.

Newstead Abbey

On Day 42, swimmer Samuel Van de Schootbrugge carried the Torch into the grounds of Newstead Abbey and past its medieval cloisters. The ancestral home of the poet Lord Byron, it was founded as a monastic house in the late 12th century, and to this day the house retains much of its medieval character. In 1818, Byron was forced to sell his family seat when the house fell into disrepair. The Abbey was bought by Thomas Wildman, who had inherited a fortune from plantations owned by his family in Jamaica.

RIGHT: Riding high. Torchbearer Dominick Cunningham brandishes the Olympic Torch from a cable car at The Heights of Abraham in Matlock, Derbyshire. Dominick, a gymnast who won two golds, a silver and a bronze medal at the Commonwealth Youth Games in 2011, said, 'It was just beautiful coming up to the hilltop to see everyone celebrating'.

OVERLEAF: Local schoolchildren wave Union flags from a hill as they wait for the Torch Relay to arrive outside Conisbrough Castle in South Yorkshire. Behind the party is the outer wall of the ruined keep, 29.5m high, which dates from the 12th century.

Week 6 Places

SATURDAY Lytham St Anne's • Warton • Preston • Blackburn • Accrington • Burnley • Crawshawbooth • Reedsholme • Rawtenstall • Rochdale • Heywood • Bury • Whitefield • Prestwich • Higher Broughton • Cheetham Hill • Manchester **SUNDAY** Salford • Trafford • Moss Side • Rusholme • Longsight • Levenshulme • Stockport • Ashton-under-Lyne • Oldham • Marsh • Huddersfield • Brighouse • Halifax • Bradford • Keighley • Skipton • Ilkley • Headingley • Potternewton • Harehills • Richmond Hill • Leeds **MONDAY** Leeds • Hunslet • Beeston • Morley • Batley • Dewsbury • Wakefield • Castleford • Pontefract • Ackworth • Lundwood • Cundy Cross • Barnsley • Darton • Kexbrough • Chapeltown • Ecclesfield • Parson Cross • Sheffield **TUESDAY** Sheffield • Rotherham • Templeborough • Dalton • Thrybergh • Conisbrough • Warmsworth • Doncaster • Armthorpe • Dunsville • Hatfield • Scunthorpe • Brigg • Wrawby • Immingham • Grimsby • Cleethorpes **WEDNESDAY** Grimsby • Louth • Legbourne • Withern • Maltby Le Marsh • Mablethorpe • Trusthorpe • Sutton-on-Sea • Mumby • Hogsthorpe • Ingoldmells • Winthorpe • Skegness • Wainfleet All Saints • Wrangle • Boston • Sleaford • Bracebridge Heath • Lincoln **THURSDAY** Lincoln • Saxilby • Darlton • East Markham • Tuxford • Kirton • Boughton • Edwinstowe • Mansfield • Kelham • Newark-on-Trent • Balderton • Grantham • Radcliffe-on-Trent **FRIDAY** Nottingham • Glapwell • Bolsover • Calow • Chesterfield • Matlock • Darley Dale • Bakewell • Buxton • Ashbourne • Derby

chapter 7
30 June to
6 July

Highlights

Feelings ran high on Armed Forces Day as Corporal Johnson Beharry, awarded the Victoria Cross in 2005, carried the Olympic Flame into the National Memorial Arboretum in Staffordshire. 'It's an honour to be here, but it was hard to enter the Arboretum knowing I too could have been a name on the wall,' he said. The Flame then travelled to the Black Country Living Museum in Dudley on board a 100-year-old steam narrow boat before riding on a tram at the Museum site. More than half of Tamworth's population came to see the Flame visit the historic Castle, and boy band The Wanted delighted fans en route from Derby to Birmingham. Sir Cliff Richard gave a memorable rendition of 'Congratulations' before passing the Flame on to Kiran Sahota, who lit the Celebration Cauldron in Cannon Hill Park.

Day 44 saw the Torch Relay travel to Coventry via Solihull, Shakespeare's birthplace in Stratford-upon-Avon, Warwick Castle and Kenilworth Castle. Dominic Macgowan, just 12 and the Torch Relay's youngest Torchbearer, enjoyed his moment to shine in Sparkbrook, Birmingham. At Solihull town crier Joe performed a 2012 version of his traditional cry: 'Oyez, oyez, oyez! Good citizens of Solihull, surrounding villages and hamlets ... let's greet the Olympic Torch, God Save the Queen'. In Astwood Bank Christian Robinson brought along his grandfather's Torch from the 1948 Games. 'My granddad died three months before I was born,' he explained, 'and I did this as a tribute to him.'

In Coventry, home of Olympic Torch manufacturers The Premier Group, the Flame visited Coventry Cathedral, built out of post-war ruins and celebrating its 50th anniversary in 2012. At Coventry City FC the Torch was carried by Ali Abdillahi. An 18-year-old attending Coventry City FC's academy, he was fostered by a British couple after seeking asylum from Somalia. Triathlete Tim Don, veteran of the 2000, 2004 and 2008 Olympic Games, took the Torch for a run (no swim or cycle this time!). The Flame also visited Althorp, resting place of Diana, Princess of Wales. Rugby giant Martin Johnson was spotted at the roadside in Foxton, his son raised on his huge shoulders, and the Flame approached Leicester through an amazing three-mile corridor, six people deep.

An intergalactic-themed community event marked a sensational beginning to Day 46. Chas Bishop, chief executive at the National Space Centre, described how 'Jet Pack Man, the coolest man in the world, made a roar of noise and handed the Torch over ... it was a magnificent experience.' From Leicester, the Torch Relay journeyed to Peterborough, where spectators

A Torch 'kiss' at Foxton Locks, Leicestershire. Robert Gomez, chairman of Bowden Cricket Club and an active cyclist for charity, passes the Olympic Flame to David Willson, who has encouraged families around London to host 1,000 Olympic and Paralympic family members in their homes for free during the Games. 'These families would not otherwise be able to afford to come to the Games and see their relatives compete,' he explains.

enjoyed another first when Torchbearer Lyn Hobson ran with her pet rabbit alongside. En route the Flame passed through Melton Mowbray, home of the famous pork pie, and Loughborough University, base for many British athletes. The Flame sampled two heritage railways, the Great Central Railway and the Nene Valley Railway, enjoyed its first 'kiss' between two boats on Rutland Water and paid a call at Burghley House, once the home of William Cecil, Elizabeth I's great statesman. Then it headed on to the Norfolk coast via King's Lynn, the Sandringham Estate and the seaside town of Cromer (famous for crabs and its Victorian Pier).

A day of colour and culture was heralded by trails of the five Olympic colours tumbling down Norwich Castle walls by abseilers. Day 48 saw the Relay relishing the haunts of composer Benjamin Britten and the pastel-hued beach huts of Southwold, before sailing down the River Orwell to Ipswich Marina. On the following day the Flame made its way to Southend-on-Sea where Olympic swimmer Mark Foster held it aloft. Hylands House in Chelmsford hosted the evening celebration as part of the Sparks will Fly: Essex Finale.

BELOW: A bit of loco-motion in Birmingham. Jose Antonio Cristobal, a volunteer firefighter and keen athlete from San Adrian in Spain, prepares to hand the Olympic Flame over to Susan Evans, an experienced foster carer.

RIGHT: All aboard for the Olympic Games! Kate Macfarlane from South Africa brandishes the Torch from the top deck of the stunningly restored Wolverhampton 49 tram, driven by Bob Dale, at the Black Country Living Museum in Dudley.

LEFT: Corporal Johnson Beharry, awarded the Victoria Cross in 2005 for saving the lives of his unit in Iraq by charging down an ambush, carries the Olympic Torch through the National Memorial Arboretum in Alrewas, Staffordshire. The names of almost 16,000 men and women killed in service since the end of the Second World War are inscribed inside its circular walls.

'The wide-eyed expressions of the three and four-year-olds are so telling.'

Geoff Doyle

LEFT: Children peer round the legs of soldiers forming a guard of honour to glimpse war hero Corporal Beharry as he pauses for a moment of silence at the National Memorial Arboretum on Armed Forces Day.

Moment to Shine

Sir Cliff Richard

Extraordinary levels of noise and screaming greeted senior British pop singer Sir Cliff Richard when he held the Olympic Torch. It did not go unnoticed that his 1959 UK number-one single with The Shadows, 'Travellin' Light', could have been written for the Torch Relay. Ever the showman, Sir Cliff waved to everyone and made the most of his time with the Flame, posing for pictures along the way. Nominated for his contribution to the music industry, the 71-year-old has seen more than 130 hit singles, albums and EPs make the UK Top 20 and holds the record (with Elvis Presley) as the only act to make the UK singles charts in all of its first six decades (1950s to 2000s). The singer's knighthood, bestowed in the 1995 Queen's Birthday Honours for his tireless charity work, was the first to be given to a pop star. Over his 53-year career, Sir Cliff has become a fixture of the British entertainment world.

LEFT: Congratulations ... and celebrations. Sir Cliff Richard delights the crowds with a rhythmic run during his Torch Relay slot in Birmingham.

OPPOSITE: Family crowds line the pavements, waving Union flags and hats as they wait for the arrival of the Torch Relay en route to Solihull.

'Thousands are out on the streets here. The sun is out and it's more like Rio than Redditch – the samba band is playing its heart out.'

Carson Wishart, BBC Hereford and Worcester

RIGHT: A midsummer day's dream. Outside Shakespeare's birthplace in Stratford-upon-Avon, Peter Wyatt, 83, a distinguished oarsman who competed in the Olympic Games trials finals in 1948 and 1952, passes the Flame to Camilla Hadland. Camilla, 19, was a gold medallist at the 2010 World Rowing Junior Championships. The Flame was welcomed by 'William Shakespeare' and young people involved with the education programme of the Shakespeare Birthplace Trust.

ABOVE: Georgina Harland, who won bronze in the Modern Pentathlon at Athens 2004, holds the Olympic Torch high at Warwick Castle. Built by William the Conqueror in 1068, the castle has been a landmark of the county for nearly 1,000 years. Huge crowds packed the streets to welcome the Flame to Warwickshire.

LEFT: Put out the bunting… Spectators, crowded six deep on pavements in Solihull, relish the Olympic spirit as they wait to capture their glimpse of the Torch Relay.

Moment to Shine

Melanie Easter, 36, is a supreme athlete by anyone's standards. Registered blind, Melanie swam for Great Britain and won a combined total of two golds, two silvers and a bronze medal from the Paralympic Games at Atlanta 1996 and Sydney 2000. After retiring from swimming she took up cycling and represented Great Britain at the 2007 Cycling World Championships. Then she took up triathlon and became the Paratriathlon World Champion in 2008. Now she has taken up rowing and competes for Warwick. Excelling academically, Melanie has gained three degrees and inspires others through her work as a Senior Physiotherapist for the NHS. She was nominated by her husband for 'inspiring others to rise to their own challenges and to strive to achieve their dreams'.

Travelling in Style

On Day 45 the Olympic Torch took to a canal boat to travel through the ten sections of Foxton Locks. Located on the Leicester line of the Grand Union Canal, and opened in 1814, the Locks are formed of two 'staircases', each consisting of five locks. Staircase locks are used when a canal has to negotiate a steep hill. Robert Gomez was the Torchbearer for this part of the journey. Robert was nominated for his work with the Bowden Cricket Club where he coaches the youth team and plays himself. He's also been involved in numerous fundraising activities for local charities.

ABOVE: Robert Gomez salutes onlookers after safely negotiating a ten-lock 'staircase' on a barge with the Olympic Torch on the Grand Union Canal at Foxton Locks in Leicestershire.

LEFT: Triathlete Tim Don, the only Briton to have competed in all three Olympic Triathlons since the event was included in the Sydney 2000 Games, carries the Torch up into the stands of the City of Coventry Stadium, a venue for Football during the Olympic Games.

LEFT: Dressed to impress. The statue of Lord John Douglas Montague Scott, a 19th-century landlord, Scottish MP and younger brother of the 5th Duke of Buccleuch, proudly sports an Olympic Games vest in Dunchurch. Locals traditionally clothe the statue every Christmas, and it was dressed as Queen Elizabeth on her Diamond Jubilee weekend.

BELOW: A tremendous reception greets Barbara Crowther, 58, a teacher who has inspired thousands of children with her enthusiasm for tradition, as she displays the Olympic Torch at Geddington.

'I've never seen a Mexican wave being done with umbrellas before, but it just happened here.'

Martin Borley in Kettering

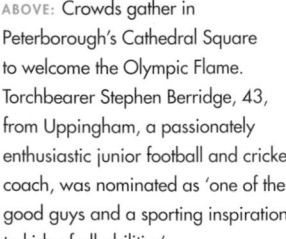

ABOVE: Crowds gather in Peterborough's Cathedral Square to welcome the Olympic Flame. Torchbearer Stephen Berridge, 43, from Uppingham, a passionately enthusiastic junior football and cricket coach, was nominated as 'one of the good guys and a sporting inspiration to kids of all abilities'.

ABOVE RIGHT: A spectator's helpful poster strikes a humorous note in Quorn, Leicestershire. The Olympic Flame travelled to Quorn & Woodhouse station on the Great Central Railway, the only double-track mainline heritage railway in the United Kingdom, in the luxurious, steam hauled Cromwell Pullman train.

RIGHT: Stuntman Eric Scott gets the day's Torch Relay action off to a flying start at the National Space Centre in Leicester. The scene was reminiscent of the Opening Ceremony at the Los Angeles 1984 Games, when a man powered by a jet pack flew into the Stadium to light the Olympic Cauldron.

ABOVE: Platform 2012. The Olympic Flame, safe in its Lantern, arrives at Orton Mere Station on Day 46. It had travelled on the Nene Valley Railway from Wandsford on board the 'City of Peterborough' steam locomotive.

LEFT: Faster, higher, stronger… An excited Jack Russell greets Torchbearer Richard Bebbington, heroic charity fundraiser, during his slot with the Olympic Torch in Leicester.

Moment to Shine

John Peake, the first Torchbearer in Peterborough, is an Olympian. John won a silver medal in the Great Britain Hockey team at London 1948 and the 87-year-old could not wait to re-live an Olympic moment. 'I am not looking forward to running the whole way – maybe I will do a jog at the start and end. It is all very exciting. I very much enjoyed being in the Olympic Games and am looking forward to seeing them in the UK again.'

'Wow
Sandringham
is so packed,
can't even move!
Everyone with
their flags. This
is why I love
England.'

Tweeted by Robert Smith

LEFT: Torchbearers Tom Collison and Philip Wilkinson exchange a Torch 'kiss' in King's Lynn's Tuesday Market Place, once the site of hangings, witch burnings and the town stocks. Tom is an active Young Farmer and Philip Wilkinson runs an inspirational office sports and social club.

RIGHT: Cromer's famous Victorian pier provides a vivid backdrop as Christina Walker passes on the Olympic Flame to Harry Heathfield. The 20-year-old volunteer first responder for the East of England Ambulance Service, who described himself as 'all hyped-up and pretty excited', then ran a double leg from the bottom of the pier to Cromer Academy.

OPPOSITE: Can everyone see the Flame? Lauren Reeder, a teaching assistant nominated as a Torchbearer by her pupils, holds the Olympic Torch up on the running track at Lynnsport and Leisure Park – just out of reach of excited young spectators.

Moment to Shine

Karen Murray, 33, was nominated as a Torchbearer by her husband Paul who says she has given everything to running her charity, Hana's Gift, in memory of her daughter Hana who was stillborn in 2006. She helps to raise funds to finance memorials, plaques and headstones for families and parents who have lost a child through late miscarriage, stillbirth or within the first year of their life. All the people she has helped so far express eternal gratitude for being able to have a memorial for their baby that they otherwise may never have been able to afford. He said, 'I think her longing to help other people who have suffered this loss while at the same time living with the pain of losing Hana makes her so special and she is such an inspiration. She is my hero and I think her work with Hana's Gift sums up the very meaning of "going the extra mile".'

'The Games haven't been here since 1948 so it's a big deal. The Flame means so much to so many people – it's great to see.'

Mel from Lowestoft

ABOVE: Up close and personal to an Olympic Torch 'kiss', you can clearly see the holes in the Torch skin. They represent the 8,000 Torchbearers who are taking the Flame on its 8,000-mile journey around the UK.

OPPOSITE: In front of Southwold's famous rainbow-coloured beach huts Richard Game, 37, hands on the Olympic Flame to Caroline Emeny. He was nominated as a Torchbearer for the 'endless hours' he devotes to keeping his community safe as a member of the Suffolk Special Constabulary.

LEFT: The figurehead. Ranvir Sandhu, 17, poised at the prow of a yacht on the River Orwell, brings the Olympic Flame safely back on to dry land at Ipswich Marina. The Flame was escorted on the river by a flotilla of small boats before an evening celebration at Christchurch Park.

ABOVE: Stephen Fenby, chartered accountant and Ironman athlete, carries the Olympic Torch along the path next to the River Wensum, in Norwich – a Site of Special Scientific Interest and a Special Conservation Area. 'My understanding of the Olympic ideal is hard work, focus, commitment, teamwork, goal setting and competition,' he said. The Flame also took a trip across the river on a rowing boat.

ABOVE RIGHT: The first Torchbearer of Day 48, Giles Long MBE, holds the Torch aloft inside Norwich Castle. A triple Paralympic gold medallist who set a world record in his 100m butterfly victory at Sydney 2000, he also overcame bone cancer after two years of treatment.

OPPOSITE: Ruling the waves. The Olympic Torch is ferried across the River Wensum in the careful hands of Elizabeth Carpenter. The boat was serenaded by cheers from the local rowing club and a rendition of 'Rule Britannia' from the Norwich Philharmonic choir.

LEFT: Marc Grayston proudly holds the Olympic Torch aloft at Basildon Sporting Village in Essex, where he completed a lap of the swimming pool and the running track. Marc runs the local karate club in Basildon, where his enthusiasm and strong bond with youngsters has seen membership increase sixfold.

BELOW: Running in the rain. Gemma Flaxman, 16, smiles through the summer downpour as she enjoys her run with the Torch through Southend-on-Sea. A fundraiser for several charities, Gemma also works with Cybermentors to support those suffering from online bullying. Her ambition is to train as a paediatrician or a psychiatrist.

ABOVE: Spectators gather in front of a colourful fairground to welcome the Flame to Southend-on-Sea. Sonia Richards, organiser of a well-received 13-week football programme for underprivileged children in East London, carries the Torch through the cheering crowds along the seafront.

RIGHT: Countdown to the Games. Emily Rogers, 18, gazes up at the Olympic Flame at Christchurch Mansion, a magnificent Tudor brick house close to Ipswich in Suffolk. She was joined on the balcony of the historic house by Tommy Smith, the international footballer who plays for both Ipswich Town and New Zealand.

OVERLEAF: Giles Long MBE, a triple Paralympic gold medallist, carries the Olympic Flame as abseilers descend down the side of Norwich Castle trailing smoke in the colours of the five Olympic rings at the start of Day 48.

Week 7 Places

SATURDAY Derby • Burton upon Trent • Streethay • Lichfield • Hopwas • Tamworth • Great Wyrley • Newtown • Bloxwich • Leamore • Birchills • Walsall • Willenhall • Wolverhampton • Dudley • Oldbury • West Bromwich • Smethwick • Birmingham **SUNDAY** Birmingham • Solihull • Earlswood • Redditch • Astwood Bank • Alcester • Evesham • Wickhamford • Broadway • Chipping Campden • Newbold on Stour • Alderminster • Stratford-upon-Avon • Warwick • Royal Leamington Spa • Kenilworth • Coventry **MONDAY** Coventry • Rugby • Dunchurch •Northampton • Wellingborough • Isham • Kettering • Geddington • Corby • Dingley • Market Harborough • Lubenham • Foxton • Kibworth Harcourt • Oadby • Leicester **TUESDAY** Leicester • Quorn • Loughborough • Hoton • Wymeswold • Asfordby • Melton Mowbray • Langham • Oakham • Uppingham • Stamford • Peterborough

WEDNESDAY Peterborough • Market Deeping • Thurlby • Bourne • Spalding • Moulton • Whaplode • Holbeach • Long Sutton • King's Lynn • South Wootton • West Rudham • East Rudham • Fakenham • Holt • Cromer • Aylsham • Norwich **THURSDAY** Norwich • Acle • Filby • Great Yarmouth • Lowestoft • Wrentham • Reydon • Southwold • Kelsale • Saxmundham • Aldeburgh • Wickham Market • Ufford • Melton • Woodbridge • Felixstowe • Ipswich

FRIDAY Ipswich • Colchester • Hatfield Peverel • Heybridge • Maldon • Rayleigh • Southend-on-Sea • Hadleigh • Basildon • Grays • Herongate • Brentwood • Chelmsford

chapter 8
7 to 13 July

Highlights

The Olympic Flame was greeted by the highest in the land this week: the Queen and the Prime Minister. Moesha Howard, an up-and-coming hurdler, launched the Flame's latest incredible journey from Ruskin University as it proceeded from Chelmsford to Cambridge. Team GB junior canoeist Zachary Franklin held the Torch aloft as he carried it down the rapids at the Lee Valley White Water Centre in Waltham Cross. Jamie Oliver whet appetites running close to where he first cooked in his parents' pub, and Olympic silver medallist Iwan Thomas sprinted the final leg to light the Celebration Cauldron at Parker's Piece, Cambridge.

On Day 51 Torchbearer Alice Ellison recreated the famous race around Trinity Great Court featured in the film 'Chariots of Fire'. Wellwishers shrugged off torrential rain on the banks of the River Cam to glimpse the Flame glide by on a punt towards Magdalene Bridge. Torchbearers included wheelchair badminton champion Gobi Ranganathan, Olympic Sailing gold medallist Sarah Gosling, Queens Park Rangers Chairman Tony Fernandes and Rifleman Michael Swain, who lost both legs serving in Helmand province in 2009. The Flame added the Jacobean estate of Hatfield House to an impressive list of stately homes visited.

Before the Flame entered his see, the Bishop of Bedford blessed the route and celebrated Olympic values. Many of his parishioners hosted events in Bedfordshire, Hertfordshire and Buckinghamshire. Lewis Hamilton, disappointed at the British Grand Prix, relished pole position as first Torchbearer in Luton. The Flame toured Bletchley Park, Britain's famous decryption centre during the Second World War, and made an emotional stop at Stoke Mandeville, site of the first International Wheelchair Games, forerunner of the Paralympic Games, in 1948. Oxfordshire provided a dash of magic with a game of Quidditch before the Flame travelled on to Blenheim Palace and Woodstock, where the Prime Minister greeted his nominated Torchbearer.

Day 53 was regal in every element. Sir Roger Bannister, 83, carried the Flame in Oxford's Iffley Road Stadium – the very place where, in 1954, he became the first 'miler' to break the four-minute barrier. In Henley-on-Thames Sir Steve Redgrave rowed the Torch one-handed in an eight, crewed by local youngsters and coxed by Garry Herbert, Olympic gold medal winner with the Searle brothers in 1992. Chefs Heston Blumenthal and Raymond Blanc added gourmet flavour to a street party celebration, while in Windsor the Queen and the Duke of Edinburgh welcomed the Flame into the Castle. London

2012 Chair Seb Coe introduced the royal party to local schoolchildren, brandishing impressive homemade 'Torches'.

Highlights on the Reading to Salisbury leg of the Relay included Olympic gymnast George Weedon, 92, who completed his role as Torchbearer 64 years after representing Britain in the 1948 Olympic Games. Brenda Heys finished her slot in a four-strong human chain, linked to her two sons, who have Down's Syndrome, and a Torch Security Team member. BBC Sports presenter Clare Balding, patron of the British Paralympic Association, carried the Torch along Northbrook Street in Newbury, among crowds ten deep. In Winchester the Flame visited the Cathedral, resting place of novelist Jane Austen, before setting off for its evening destination, home of another glorious cathedral, Salisbury.

A dawn visit to Stonehenge with sprint legend Michael Johnson began a memorable Day 55, the Flame returning from the prehistoric stones to Salisbury's Cathedral Green. In Barford St Martin, primary school teacher Gemma David added Morris dancing to the Torchbearer repertoire. The Torch visited Shaftesbury, passed regimental badges etched into the chalk hillside outside Fovant and wound through beautiful Thomas Hardy country to Dorchester. The week ended against the stunning backdrop of the Jurassic Coast, taking in Lyme Bay, home of the Olympic Sailing events, and the striped lighthouse at Pulpit Rock before reaching Bournemouth's sandy beaches for a splendid evening event.

Frankie Dettori leaps from the saddle of ex-racehorse Monsignor with his trademark starfish victory salute. He and Monsignor carried the Olympic Flame around the parade ring at Ascot Racecourse, Berkshire, where the jockey made history in 1996 by winning all seven races in one day.

LEFT: Mark Reynolds holds the ashes of his brother David, who suffered from Duchenne's Muscular Dystrophy. David had been nominated as a London 2012 Torchbearer, but sadly died in February, so Mark took his place. 'I am running in his honour,' said Mark. 'He made everybody who met him laugh and smile.'

BELOW: The Olympic Flame is held in its Lantern by a Torch Security Team member at the Imperial War Museum Duxford. The museum, set in the grounds of the famous former First and Second World War airfield, is home to more than two hundred aircraft as well as tanks, military vehicles and boats.

Travelling in Style

On Day 50 the Flame paid a visit to the Lee Valley White Water Centre, venue for the five-day Olympic Games Canoe Slalom competition. Zachary Franklin, a British team junior canoeist and Olympic hopeful, had the honour of carrying the Torch down the course before 2,000 spectators. Led by their captain Paskell Blackwell, the full Great Britain Senior Men's White Water Rafting team paddled through the swirling currents. The Centre will be the first brand new London 2012 venue to open to the public after the Games.

Moment to Shine

Jamie Oliver
appeared on the Torch Relay schedule just before lunchtime, pukka in his whites (of the Torchbearer uniform variety, not his kitchen garb). He was running with the Torch in the village of Newport, close to where he first cooked at his parents' pub. Selected for inspiring people to enjoy spending more time in the kitchen and to start growing their own food, he has campaigned vocally against the use of processed food in national schools. His Jamie Oliver Foundation is a charity which aims to empower, educate and inspire people to love and enjoy good food, as well as fight against obesity.

'I'm actually running past my old school and finishing near the local pub that we used to escape to, so it's sort of ironic really, but nice,' he said. 'I was born near Southend and I grew up in north Essex here in Saffron Waldon and I love it. It's a good county. It's got lots to offer. Essex is still in my heart.'

ABOVE: Walking tall. Stilt walkers dressed in imaginative Union flag designs cheer on the Olympic Flame from their vantage point in Chelmsford.

ABOVE: Ready, steady, Flame… Jamie Oliver celebrates with the Flame close to his parents' pub in Newport, Essex, where he first learned to cook. 'I'm just going to ham it up and rinse it for every step,' he promised.

Edward Roberts, volunteer and community worker, holds the Olympic Torch aloft as he reclines in a punt on the River Cam. The punt travelled past St John's College and under the intricate Bridge of Sighs on to Magdalene Bridge, in torrential rain.

FAR LEFT: Another iconic scene from the film 'Chariots of Fire' is re-created by Torchbearer Alice Ellison, aged 18. She ran around the perimeter of the Great Court in Trinity College, Cambridge, a distance said to have been run by athlete David Burghley in around 43 seconds (the time it takes for the clock to strike 12). Alice was nominated for her role as a Young Ambassador for the Cambridge School Sports Partnership and her sporting achievements.

LEFT: The Jacobean magnificence of Hatfield House, the home of the seventh Marquess and Marchioness of Salisbury, provides a stunning backdrop for the Olympic Flame. Alice Breheny carried the Torch in honour of her late sister and father, both of whom died of brain tumours.

209

'I'm so honoured to have been asked to carry the Torch. Never in a million years did I think I'd get to do something so cool.'

Formula One driver Lewis Hamilton

OPPOSITE: Spectators flock to Blenheim Palace, home to the 11th Duke and Duchess of Marlborough and birthplace of Sir Winston Churchill, in Woodstock, West Oxfordshire. 'We are honoured and delighted that the Olympic Torch Relay has come to Blenheim Palace,' said His Grace the 11th Duke of Marlborough. 'I am especially pleased that there are over 3,000 children here today.'

RIGHT: Pole position. Formula One driver Lewis Hamilton swaps the front row of the starting grid for the 001 Torchbearer badge as he prepares to rev up Torch Relay action in Luton. Hamilton was due to run through his home town of Stevenage, but a clash with the British Grand Prix at Silverstone meant he ran in Luton instead.

FAR RIGHT: Hazel Staten, a leukaemia survivor, holds the Olympic Torch at Bletchley Park. The nation's top-secret centre of code-breaking during the Second World War, Bletchley is now a museum.

ABOVE: The Torch Relay Circus. Jodie Evans lives life to the full despite suffering from Multiple Sclerosis. She carried the Olympic Torch outside the Mini factory in Oxford, hotly pursued by one of its products.

RIGHT: Carnival queen. Luton was packed with spectators early in the morning, intent on celebrating the Olympic Flame's presence with style and energy.

LEFT: Torchbearer Sarah Winckless paddles the Flame along Eton Dorney Lake, site of the Rowing, Paralympic Rowing and Canoe Sprint events at London 2012. Sarah, a world champion and Olympic Games bronze medallist for Rowing, is now Chair of the British Olympic Association's Athletes' Commission.

BELOW: Excited crowds line The Long Walk, an avenue of trees stretching from Windsor Castle to Snow Hill, to enjoy the atmosphere as the Torch is carried through.

'The crowd are going absolutely wild. I'd never realised that I would actually feel choked up. I now feel like I'm part of the spirit of the Olympic Games. It's absolutely electric.'

Kat Orman, BBC Radio Oxford

Moment to Shine

Sir Roger Bannister, 83, carried the Torch at the Iffley Road track in Oxford to begin Day 53. At the track, now renamed after him, Bannister was the first athlete to break the four-minute mile barrier on 6 May 1954. The former runner who became a distinguished neurologist and Master of Pembroke College, Oxford, said of his moment, 'It brings back happy memories and also brings back some of the weather. Today it looks like it might rain and that day the weather was so bad that I nearly decided not to attempt it. In retrospect I'm glad because if I hadn't that day, I might not have had another chance.' Seb Coe added, 'Breaking the four-minute mile as a mark of athletic achievement sits central in the history of our sport. He paved the way for what we did in the late 70s and early 80s.'

OPPOSITE: Royal approval. HRH Queen Elizabeth II and the Duke of Edinburgh greet rain-soaked Torchbearer Gina MacGregor – awarded the MBE for services to netball, which she has played for 65 years – and London 2012 Chair Seb Coe outside Windsor Castle.

LEFT: The history man. Sir Roger Bannister passes on the Olympic Flame at Iffley Road Stadium, Oxford, on the very track where, in 1954, he became the first man to run a mile in under four minutes.

BELOW: Star of Sydney 2000. Denise Lewis, Heptathlon gold medallist, re-enacts an Olympic Games lap of honour around the parade ring at Ascot Racecourse, Berkshire.

BELOW: Sir Steve Redgrave, Britain's greatest Olympian, rows one-handed past the Leander Club, Henley-on-Thames. The eight was crewed by up-and-coming young rowers and coxed by Garry Herbert, who won a gold medal with the Searle brothers in 1992.

OPPOSITE: Party spirit. Jovial spectators wave Union flags and salute the arrival of the Olympic Flame as the Torch Relay travels between Amesbury and Salisbury.

'To have my hands on the Torch is pretty special. When I retired in 2000 I was asked to come on to the bid team. What we were working towards were the Games in 2012 and now it's just 18 days away.'

Sir Steve Redgrave, five-time gold medal winning Olympian

Moment to Shine

George Weedon

Reliving memories of 1948, Olympic gymnast George Weedon, who represented Great Britain in the last home Games, took his turn as Torchbearer in Reading. He described being reunited with the sight of the Olympic Flame as 'overwhelming', adding, 'I loved meeting my fellow Torchbearers on the bus, talking and exchanging stories about our life experiences. Everybody had lots of questions about 1948, when we went to work first and were amateur athletes second.'

George, now a sprightly 92, participated in the Team All-Round, Floor Exercise, Horse Vault, Parallel Bars, Horizontal Bar, Rings and Pommel Horse. 'It was just after the war and we had no gyms,' he laughed. 'I used to train by doing free running and challenging myself by climbing lamp posts and using telegraph poles and hoardings as apparatus.'

Clare Balding, set to host much of the BBC Olympic Games coverage, carries the Olympic Torch through the thronged streets of Newbury. Later she tweeted, 'That was absolutely AMAZING. I was in bits getting off the bus … Thank you Newbury!'

Spencer Whatmore, from Chichester, was nominated for being an all-round 'good egg' who works to improve the confidence of excluded children and those with special educational needs. He holds the Torch aloft in the midst of the Olympic rings formed by children in coloured T-shirts.

BELOW LEFT: How excited are we? Jubilant young spectators give the Flame an uproarious welcome in Kings Worthy, Hampshire.

LEFT: Kirstie Nash, 17, nominated for her ability to juggle caring for her disabled sister with full-time study, passes the Olympic Flame to Phillip Blowfield, a stalwart village fundraiser who has just retired from Thames Valley Police, outside Winchester Cathedral.

OVERLEAF: Gold on gold. Sprint legend Michael Johnson is silhouetted against the rising sun as he holds the Flame between two standing stones at Stonehenge on Salisbury Plain, Wiltshire.

'Sun's out, sun's rising, clear skies today and running with the Torch around Stonehenge was an incredible moment.'

Michael Johnson, 400m record holder

LEFT: Getting hands-on. On the Green outside Salisbury Cathedral, schoolgirls from Leadenhall School, Salisbury crowd round to touch the Olympic Torch carried by all-star long-sprint legend Michael Johnson.

ABOVE: Jack Delaney, a passionate supporter of Southampton FC, leads the Torch Relay convoy through Blandford Forum, Wiltshire. He is an ambassador for a charity which takes disabled and disadvantaged children to sporting and cultural events. 'My dream for the future is to ensure that as many disabled and disadvantaged children as possible will have the opportunity to experience a fantastic day out watching their football or music hero,' he says.

LEFT: Alan Surtees MBE, the cycling advisor to the Duke of Edinburgh Awards scheme, proudly brandishes the Olympic Torch at the top of Gold Hill in Shaftesbury, Dorset. The steep cobbled street became famous for its role in Hovis Bakery advertisements.

OPPOSITE: 'Flame ahoy!' Torch Relay fans seen in silhouette perched on a ship's mast as they watch Andrew Clutton carry the Olympic Torch between Hamworthy and Poole.

OVERLEAF: Lisa Devine, 15, selected for her dedication to the Swim Bournemouth performance squad and her youth ambassador work, carries the Olympic Flame up the cliffs from Durdle Door in Dorset. The natural limestone arch forms part of the Jurassic Coast.

ABOVE: Toby Gutteridge carries the Olympic Flame through Branksome in Dorset. Toby fulfilled his lifelong dream to join the Special Boat Service in 2009, but was shot in the neck on his first tour of duty. He has set a great example of courage and determination.

ABOVE RIGHT: Lining the streets. Crowds gather excitedly behind a giant Union flag anticipating the arrival of the Olympic Flame in Poole, Dorset.

RIGHT: Victoria Mattock, a fundraiser for Acorns Children's Hospice, displays the Olympic Torch from a hill overlooking Portland and the long curve of Chesil Beach. She was nominated for her charity work by Lloyds TSB.

Week 8 Places

SATURDAY Chelmsford • Harlow • Waltham Abbey • Waltham Cross • Hertford • Ware • Bishop's Stortford • Stansted Mountfitchet • Newport • Saffron Walden • Haverhill • Bury St Edmunds • Newmarket • Cambridge

SUNDAY Cambridge • St Ives • Huntingdon • Bedford • Cotton End • Letchworth Garden City • Stevenage • Welwyn Garden City • Hatfield • St Albans • Hemel Hempstead • Luton **MONDAY** Luton • Dunstable • Milton Keynes • Bletchley • Buckingham • Winslow • Whitchurch • Aylesbury • Stoke Mandeville • Aylesbury • Waddesdon • Bicester • Kirtlington • Woodstock • Kidlington • Oxford **TUESDAY** Oxford • Abingdon • Wallingford • Crowmarsh Gifford • Nettlebed • Henley-on-Thames • Bisham (Bisham Abbey) • Maidenhead • Slough • Windsor • Egham • Ascot • Bracknell • Reading **WEDNESDAY** Reading • Theale • Thatcham • Newbury • Basingstoke • Kings Worthy • Winchester • Andover • Ludgershall • Tidworth • Amesbury • The Winterbournes • Salisbury **THURSDAY** Salisbury • Wilton • Barford St Martin • Fovant • Ludwell • Shaftesbury • Fontmell Magna • Iwerne Minster • Stourpaine • Blandford Forum • Winterborne • Whitechurch • Milborne St Andrew • Puddletown • Dorchester • Winterbourne Abbas • Bridport • Chideock • Lyme Regis • Burton Bradstock • Abbotsbury • Portesham • Chickerell • Wyke Regis • Osprey Quay, Portland • Weymouth **FRIDAY** Portland Bill • Southwell • Weston • Easton • Portland • Fortuneswell • Weymouth • Preston • Osmington • Winfrith Newburgh • Wool • Corfe Castle • Swanage • Stoborough • Wareham • Sandford • Lytchett Minster • Upton • Hamworthy • Poole • Ashley Cross • Branksome • Wallisdown • Bournemouth

Chapter 9
14 to 20 July

Highlights

Seaside fun was the theme as the Torch Relay set off from Bournemouth Pier on Saturday morning, winding its way through the New Forest to Lymington, then boarding a ferry to the Isle of Wight. Strong winds welcomed the Flame, as Torchbearers gingerly transported it up and down The Needles Chairlift at Alum Bay beach. Sailors were much in evidence; Shirley Robertson, double Olympic gold medallist, navigated the streets of Newport, while solo long-distance yachtswoman Dame Ellen MacArthur delighted crowds in East Cowes. A sortie to Osborne House, Queen Victoria's favourite summer residence, provided an inland highlight.

Back across the Solent, the Flame was exchanged pitchside at St Mary's Stadium, Southampton. After a lap of honour, it headed on to Portsmouth by the most scenic route imaginable – via Guernsey and Jersey, on board BA2012 'The Firefly'. In Guernsey the first Torchbearer was retired surgeon Roger Allsopp, 71, the oldest person to swim the Channel, who carried the Torch along South Esplanade in St Peter Port.

Special Olympics cycling gold medallist Jamie Bichard took the Flame past Guernsey Lighthouse, serenaded by the Guernsey Chansonelles Choir. In Jersey, a highly charged festive atmosphere saw the Flame progress from Bel Royal along the seafront to St Helier and a celebratory Cauldron at the Weighbridge. Back on the mainland, the Flame travelled from Gosport to the Historic dockyard at Portsmouth, where it boarded HMS Victory.

Day 59 kicked off with John Jenkins, 92, a fan of 50 years' standing who brought the Olympic spirit to the pitch at Portsmouth Football Club. The Relay stopped at Petworth House, Sussex, to admire the 17th-century architecture and 700-acre deer park, before taking in the Cass Sculpture Park in Goodwood and Arundel Castle. The athletic figures of Sally Biggs, née Gunnell, a 400m Hurdles gold medallist, and Robin Cousins, who won gold in men's Figure Skating, recalled past Olympic glories in Bognor Regis and Brighton.

From Brighton's Pavilion the Flame moved on and enjoyed performances galore at a lively evening celebration hosted by Hastings. On Day 60 it reached the Kent coast via Tonbridge Castle, where Dame Kelly Holmes, the 1500m and 800m gold medallist at Athens 2004, and Frank Verge, a Torchbearer in the 1948 Relay, displayed the Flame to a delighted crowd. Otherwise it was a day of Eddies – former stunt rider Eddie Kidd roared off on his Torchbearing leg in Lewes, while comedian Eddie Izzard won applause in Bexhill-on-Sea.

A day of photogenic motion beckoned on Day 61. The Flame travelled up and down the East Hill Cliff Railway in Hastings, visited the entrance of the Channel Tunnel and sailed on a tall ship into Dover, having been delivered by a RNLI lifeboat from Samphire Hoe. The following day it touched Deal Pier and explored the grounds of Canterbury Cathedral before arriving at Leeds Castle in Maidstone. Among the Torchbearers were javelin Olympic medallist Steve Backley, swimmer Karen Pickering, tennis player Elena Baltacha and artist Tracy Emin, who described her day as 'the most surreal dream you can ever imagine'.

Day 63 saw a dramatic 105-mile journey from Maidstone to Guildford. A crew from Maidstone Rowing Club took the Flame on the water, followed by a bike ride around the famous Brands Hatch racing track. Bells rang to welcome the Flame at a chain of ancient churches in Surrey: St Nicholas's at Godstone, St Mary's at Bletchingley and St Martin's at Dorking. Olympian Torchbearer Roger Black shone in front of Godalming crowds, commemorating his 14 years as a GBR athlete in which he won three Olympic medals, two silver and one bronze.

At dusk, in a spectacular end to the week, a Royal Navy Sea King helicopter set off from Guildford and Marine Martyn Williams abseiled with the Olympic Flame into the Tower of London. After a reception to celebrate the Flame's arrival in the capital, it was secured overnight in a vault which also houses London 2012's medals.

James Bond, eat your heart out. Royal Marine Martyn Williams coolly abseils from a Royal Navy Sea King helicopter over Tower Bridge. He brought the Olympic Flame into the Tower of London, where it spent its first night in the capital.

The Needles Park and Chairlift

The Needles Park Chairlift is known for its 'scariness' factor and is thus a firm favourite for family visitors to see the Isle of Wight's most famous landmark. The Olympic Flame rode in one of the 50 chairs from the clifftop amusement park down to the pebbly Alum Bay Beach and back. The views are truly spectacular – the five iconic chalk stacks that comprise the Needles Rocks, the lighthouse that since 1959 has warned seafarers making their way up the Solent of the rock hazards, the multi-coloured sand cliffs and often stunningly turquoise sea.

Sky high. David Ouston, 46, who set up Street Pastors on the Isle of Wight to be 'a light in the darkness' and help people in need, brandishes the Olympic Flame on The Needles Park Chairlift.

ABOVE: A lap of honour. Alice Constance, 30, carries the Olympic Flame around St. Mary's Stadium in her home town of Southampton to thunderous applause. A member of the Serpentine swimmers, she is also a triathlete and has completed a heroic swim across the Channel.

LEFT: One for the record. Claire Gunn, a Metropolitan Police Torch Security officer, heralds the Olympic Flame's arrival by ferry into Southampton.

OVERLEAF: Torchbearer Annette Ablitt holds the Olympic Torch proudly aloft on her slot between Carisbrooke and East Cowes. A carer for her partner who suffers from the incurable Huntington's disease, she also finds time for voluntary teaching and charity work.

'If you're thinking it's just a Flame and no big deal, change your mind. The atmosphere and welcome for the Torch Relay is electric.'

Neil Sackley, BBC

ABOVE: Yingliang Zhu, an electronic power worker from Shanghai, leaps with excitement as he carries the Olympic Torch through Totland. He was nominated as a Torchbearer for his promotion of the concept of low-carbon, energy saving and environment protection.

OPPOSITE: Mazie Watson, 12, enjoys a Torch 'kiss' with Colette Hayes in front of local dignitaries in Portsmouth. Mazie carried the Torch from the jetty at the Historic Dockyard to HMS Victory, the flagship used by Lord Nelson at the Battle of Trafalgar, after the Flame travelled across the Solent on the Gosport Ferry.

ABOVE: The Flame has landed. Deborah Hale, Olympic Torch Relay Producer, carries the Olympic Flame off BA2012 'The Firefly' to a warm welcome in the Channel Islands.

LEFT: A member of the Torch Security Team presents the Lantern holding the Olympic Flame in Portsmouth. The famous Spinnaker Tower in the background affords incredible views over Portsmouth Harbour and its environs.

'In Petersfield the music is playing, kids are dancing, the bunting is out and the cobbled high street is packed with people.'

Jo Palmer, BBC Radio Solent

OPPOSITE: Colourful bunting celebrates the Olympic Flame's joyful procession through the streets of St Peter Port in Guernsey.

ABOVE LEFT: Extra time. John Jenkins, a 92-year-old veteran of the Normandy landings in the Second World War, displays the Olympic Flame at Fratton Park. He attended his first match in 1928 and has worked for Portsmouth Football Club for over 50 years, latterly as a much loved steward.

ABOVE RIGHT: Thousands turned out to create tunnels of support for the runners carrying the Olympic Flame through Hove. It arrived in the afternoon of Day 59 via Chichester, Bognor, Arundel, Worthing and Lancing.

RIGHT: A dream come true. Paul Zetter takes the Olympic Flame through Cass Sculpture Park, on the Goodwood Estate, West Sussex. He was the first chairman of SportsAid from 1976 to 1985, when the charity was the main source of funding for all amateur British athletes.

BELOW RIGHT: Hip, hip, hooray. A mass of excited schoolchildren prepare to give the Olympic Torch Relay a high-decibel reception at Petworth House, West Sussex.

FAR RIGHT: Clare Forbes, 28, proudly carries the Olympic Torch through Lancing. She contracted meningitis at the age of 17, losing both legs, some fingers and suffering a brain injury which leaves her constantly dizzy. Nevertheless the mother-of-two has completed both London and New York Marathons as well as many other fundraising challenges.

The Seven Sisters cliffs in East Sussex form a dramatic backdrop for Kathy Gore's run with the Olympic Torch at Seaford Head. An inspirational fundraiser for Sussex Hospices, she is admired for her willingness 'to go that extra mile for community and county'.

OPPOSITE: A sea of faces gives a resounding welcome to famous old girl Dame Kelly Holmes, who took the Olympic Flame at Tonbridge Castle. The double gold medallist was delighted with the support given by pupils from Hildenborough School. 'The Olympic spirit for me is just massive and the Flame has captured everyone's imagination,' she declared.

LEFT: Eddie Izzard, actor, comedian and marathon runner, dons the Torchbearer uniform as part of a contingent of runners carrying the Flame from Pevensey to Bexhill-on-Sea, where he grew up. Behind him a bus installation from the Cultural Olympiad pays homage to the classic film 'The Italian Job'.

BELOW LEFT: A milestone moment. Torchbearer Vanessa Burns runs with a huge smile through the centre of Tunbridge Wells, relishing her newfound athletic freedom after pioneering leg surgery.

Moment to Shine

Vanessa Burns,
15, achieved her aim to inspire other children born with a rare birth defect called proximal femoral focal deficiency with her run with the Olympic Torch along the famous colonnade in Tunbridge Wells. Vanessa was born with one leg shorter than the other. Just months ago, she could not walk properly, unable to put both feet flat on the floor. After undergoing pioneering surgery in France to lengthen her left thigh bone by almost 9cm, straighten the bone and correct knee problems, she is now building up her muscles so she can dance, run and enjoy her new freedom.

ABOVE: A shining light. Graham Hutchison carefully takes the Flame inside historic Dover Castle, whose massive stone walls were started in the 1160s by Henry II. Graham brightens numerous lives by being passionate about helping others with voluntary school, student and conservation projects.

ABOVE RIGHT: Who's come to see who? A carnival of larger-than-life puppets linger on the pavement in the village of Hamstreet, close to Ashford in Kent, delighting the crowds waiting for the Torch Relay to arrive.

Moment to Shine

Bernard Af Forselles, 44, local hero and eccentric, holds two official Guinness World records for running the fastest marathons in fancy dress – first as a leprechaun and then as a Viking. The latter he achieved at the London Marathon in 2011 to raise funds for a local wild animal park and to raise awareness of the desperate plight of some endangered animals. The person who nominated him wrote that 'Ben combines a great sense of fun with a deeply held desire to help those less fortunate, whether human or animal. I think he embodies the spirit of the Olympic Games.'

OPPOSITE: Alison Ward, 29, carries the Torch through Samphire Hoe at the entrance of the Channel Tunnel, which opened in 1994. She was nominated for single-mindedly putting '1000 per cent effort' into sponsored charity events and running the 'Sunshine Club' for children with special needs.

RIGHT: Latvian Linda Klavina, 13, lives with a foster family in an SOS Children's Village (which provides loving homes for orphaned or abandoned children). Here she shows her burgeoning athletic talent as she takes the Torch along the coastal path between Samphire Hoe and Dover.

ABOVE: Triple Olympic medallist Steven Backley competed in the Javelin Throw at four Games from 1992 to 2004. 'A few people are nervous I'm going to throw the Torch, but I promise I won't be tempted,' he laughed on his stint through Ramsgate.

RIGHT: The Torch Security Team prepare to transfer the Olympic Flame into its Lantern before the Torch Relay breaks for lunch at Westgate-on-Sea. Handing over the Flame is Daniel O'Donovan, 60, a PE teacher and head teacher passionate about school sport. He has devoted his life to young people in Kent.

ABOVE: Thomas Clues, 18, spreads the Olympic spirit as he carries the Torch through Canterbury. Born with cystic fibrosis, he inspires everyone with his love of life and dramatic talent.

'Totally AMAZING experience! Can't describe it. Just buzzing!'

Karen Pickering, Britain's first swimming world champion

ABOVE LEFT: Tracey Emin, one of 12 artists who have created posters for the Olympic and Paralympic Games, raises the Olympic Flame inside the Turner Contemporary Gallery in her hometown of Margate, alongside 'The Kiss' sculpture by Rodin.

ABOVE RIGHT: The stuff that dreams are made of. Young spectators enjoy the camaraderie and flag waving celebrations as they cheer on the Torch Relay in St Lawrence, Kent.

BELOW: Ashley Jackson, Team GB Hockey star, passes the Olympic Flame to 15-year-old sports fan Matthew Church outside the Guru Nanak Marg Gundwara. The temple, in Saddington Street, Gravesend is the largest place of worship for the Sikh community in the UK.

BELOW RIGHT: The Maidstone Rowing Club take the Olympic Flame for a ride on a replica royal barge on the River Medway. Torchbearer David Boyle, a Salvation Army officer, received a huge cheer as he took the Flame on board, in a colourful start to Day 63.

'That was absolutely amazing to be part of the Torch Relay ... For me this is massive.'

Craig Preece, war veteran and Brands Hatch Torchbearer

ABOVE: Swinging into town. Royal Marine Martyn Williams gives the Flame a grand entrance into the capital, descending from a helicopter by the Olympic rings on Tower Bridge.

RIGHT: Power and pride. Craig Preece, a soldier whose leg was amputated following injury when serving in Afghanistan, emerges from the pit leg at Brands Hatch on his mountain bike to carry the Olympic Flame around the race track. 'That was phenomenal,' he said.

Travelling in Style

At 20.12 BST, on Day 63, the Olympic Flame was abseiled into the Tower of London from a Royal Navy Sea King helicopter. Royal Marine Martyn Williams passed on the Flame to Dame Kelly Holmes, who took it on to the ancient ramparts of the Tower. Abul Kasam, 30, a voluntary worker in the borough of Tower Hamlets, presented the Flame to guests at a reception in the Jewel House. The Flame took part in the Tower's ancient Ceremony of the Keys before being taken to the Queen's House for overnight safekeeping by General The Lord Dannatt, Constable of the Tower of London.

LOCOG Chair Seb Coe described the Tower as a fitting entry point for the Olympic Flame to arrive in the host city: 'It is where the significance of the Monarch resides, while it also houses London 2012's medals.'

Mayor of London Boris Johnson jokingly remarked, 'As Henry VIII discovered, with at least two of his wives, it was the perfect place to bring an old flame!'

OVERLEAF: Zachary Narvaez, 17, who has raised £4,000 for cancer research, poses with the Olympic Torch outside the Royal Pavilion in his home town of Brighton.

Week 9 Places

SATURDAY Bournemouth • Boscombe • Christchurch • Lyndhurst • Brockenhurst • Lymington • Totland • Yarmouth • Carisbrooke • Newport • East Cowes • Southampton **SUNDAY** Southampton • St Peter Port • St Helier • Fareham • Bridgemary • Gosport • Portsmouth **MONDAY** Portsmouth • Petersfield • Rogate • Midhurst • Easebourne • Tillington • Petworth • Duncton • Chichester • North Bersted • South Bersted • Bognor Regis • Woodgate • Westergate • Arundel • Worthing • Lancing • West Blatchington • Brighton & Hove **TUESDAY** Brighton & Hove • Crawley • Copthorne • Felbridge • East Grinstead • Royal Tunbridge Wells • Crowborough • Lewes • Eastbourne • Pevensey Bay • Pevensey • Bexhill-on-Sea • St Leonards-on-Sea • Hastings **WEDNESDAY** Hastings • Rye • Hamstreet • Ashford • Hythe • Sandgate • Folkestone • Dover **THURSDAY** Deal • Sholden • Sandwich • Great Stonar • Cliffsend • St Lawrence • Ramsgate • Broadstairs • St Peters • Cliftonville • Margate • Westgate-on-Sea • Birchington • Upstreet • Sturry • Canterbury • Thanington • Faversham • Challock • Harrietsham • Maidstone **FRIDAY** Maidstone • Chatham • Gillingham • Rochester • Higham • Gravesend • Borough Green • Seal • Sevenoaks • Riverhead • Godstone • Bletchingley • Redhill • Reigate • Dorking • Westcott • Shere • Godalming • Guildford

Chapter 10
21 to 27 July

Highlights

In Week 10 the Flame embarked on its circuit of London, criss-crossing the capital's 33 boroughs in blazing sunshine. Every minute of Days 64 to 70 drew gasps of admiration, brought joy, instilled tears, thrilled children and prompted zealous celebrations. As Mayor of London Boris Johnson said, 'The excitement is growing so much that the Geiger counter of Olympomania is going "zoink" off the scale.'

The Flame's journey through London started at the Royal Greenwich Observatory. Sir Robin Knox-Johnston took his Torch on to the Cutty Sark. In Woolwich the Flame was flanked by riders of the King's Troop, Royal Horse Artillery, before making a daredevil rooftop foray at North Greenwich Arena. Early morning on Day 65 saw the Flame poised on top of a pod on the London Eye, before travelling through corridors of cyclists at Redbridge, on the water at Fairlop Lake and on rails at Barking Park's miniature train line.

On the Lewisham to Wandsworth route, Doreen Lawrence projected the importance of Olympic values in carrying the Flame in memory of her son Stephen who was killed in 1993. Crystal Palace, Battersea Dogs & Cats Home and the All England Lawn Tennis Club at Wimbledon provided platforms for Marlon Devonish, Michael Owen and Andy Murray before the Flame was carried on to a soap-opera set by actor Perry Fenwick in a special live episode of 'EastEnders'. James Cracknell, Boris Becker, Michael Vaughan and Chemmy Alcott added their own sporting magic, and the Prince of Wales and the Duchess of Cornwall greeted the Torch Relay in Tottenham. The Flame also took a trip on the Tube via the District Line, and former goalkeeper Gordon Banks revivified the aura of 1966 World Cup success at Wembley. A party vibe was fed by musicians Katy B, Mark Ronson and Beverley Knight.

The last two days became a kaleidoscope of distinguished people and places. Princes William and Harry and the Duchess of Cambridge welcomed the Flame to Buckingham Palace. The Flame visited Regent's Canal, St Pancras Station, St Paul's Cathedral, the Millennium Bridge, Shakespeare's Globe, Holland Park and Downing Street. On Day 70, the final stretch of the 8,000-mile adventure, the Olympic Flame journeyed through Hampton Court Palace, visiting the famous and oldest maze in the world, before being conveyed by Olympian Matthew Pinsent on to the royal barge Gloriana. The vessel made stately progress down the Thames powered by rowers young and old. Crowds thronged the banks and waded knee-deep into the river. At 12.30pm the Gloriana arrived at Tower Bridge: the Flame had finally arrived.

It remained at City Hall until darkness fell. In an inspired touch, David Beckham piloted a speedboat on which young footballer Jade Bailey carried the Olympic Flame under Tower Bridge to the Olympic Park. He passed the Flame on to Sir Steve Redgrave to carry into the Stadium. Seven established British Olympic heroes: Lynn Davies, Duncan Goodhew, Dame Kelly Holmes, Dame Mary Peters, Shirley Robertson and Daley Thompson, along with Sir Steve, had each nominated a young Olympic hopeful. These seven young athletes were handed a Torch each, with which they lit the copper petals which form the spectacular Olympic Torch.

Each competing delegation had carried into the Olympic Stadium and laid down a copper petal inscribed with the country's name and the words 'XXX Olympiad London 2012'. The young Torchbearers used their Flames to ignite the copper petals, triggering the ignition of more than 200 further petals, one for each Olympic nation. The individual Flames spread between the petals, rising up to converge and form a Cauldron. 'It embodies a sense of generosity and graciousness,' said Danny Boyle of the symbolic coming together. The Torch Relay was over, and the Games could begin.

Glowing finale. After the Flame's 8,000-mile journey around the UK, it takes pride of place in the centre of the Olympic Stadium. It was a glorious climax to a three and a half hour Opening Ceremony, as the London 2012 Games were declared open.

ABOVE: Come on Team GB. Five-year-old Kayleigh Collins from Bow welcomes the Flame to Stepney Park draped in red, white and blue from head to toe.

RIGHT: The oldest runner in the Relay, Fauja Singh, aged 101, takes his turn with the Olympic Flame in Newham. He started his career as a marathon runner at the age of 89 and has now completed nine marathons, raising funds for various global charities.

OPPOSITE: Workmen join the celebrations as the Olympic Flame passes below with a 'look, no hands' wave from their excellent vantage point.

Moment to Shine

Nadia Comaneci

At Montreal 1976 the Romanian star delighted the world by winning three gold medals and becoming the first gymnast to score a perfect 10, aged just 14. Four years later she won two more gold medals at Moscow 1980. On Day 64 Nadia again captivated onlookers as she met former basketball star John Amaechi on the roof of the North Greenwich Arena to exchange the Flame. Wearing safety harnesses, the little and large pair gingerly walked over a portion of the roof before Amaechi boarded the Woolwich Ferry to transport the Flame across the Thames. The Arena is the venue for the London 2012 Gymnastics events and Basketball finals.

LEFT: Torchbearer Nadia Comaneci, who as a 14-year-old changed gymnastics forever with her perfect 10 scores at the 1976 Montreal Games, admires the views from the viewing platform of the North Greenwich Arena.

OPPOSITE: The Olympic Flame enjoys an outing on the miniature railway in Barking Park, escorted by Paul Freedman, aged 87. Paul was made a MBE in 2008 for his charity fundraising.

ABOVE: Nicholas Moseley, an aspiring Olympian rower, carries the Olympic Torch on a sailing boat on the 38-acre lake at Fairlop Waters Country Park in Barkingside, Essex. He was accompanied by London Youth Games sailors.

LEFT: Christine Gosden, a volunteer for Girlguiding UK, takes the Olympic Flame through beautiful gardens to the front door of Hall Place. The Grade I listed Tudor mansion, dating from 1537, was built in Bexley for a former Lord Mayor of London.

'It was amazing to look out and see the whole of London ... The height was quite scary but you know you're safe so it's not too bad.'

Amelia Hempleman-Adams, youngest person to ski to the South Pole, and London Eye Torchbearer

LEFT: Aaron Reynolds, 18, a former Royal Yacht Association Thames Valley Young Sailor of the Year and active volunteer instructor, crosses the Thames with the Olympic Torch on a London Fire Brigade Boat, leading a flotilla of small craft.

RIGHT: Ashley Banjo runs with the Olympic Flame towards the stage at the Dagenham Town Show in Central Park, Dagenham, surrounded by fellow members of dance troupe Diversity. The dynamic street dance group, Britain's Got Talent winners in 2009, are inspiring role models with their motto 'Dream, Believe, Achieve'.

OPPOSITE: Don't look now. The achievements of young adventurer Amelia Hempleman-Adams reach new heights as she brandishes the Olympic Torch on top of the London Eye. Behind her stretches a glorious view to the west, showcasing the River Thames, Westminster Bridge, the Houses of Parliament and Battersea Power Station.

Moment to Shine

Tom Traill, 25, set up and manages the charity FoodCycle, which provides volunteer cooks every Sunday at a community centre in Bromley-by-Bow. FoodCycle takes food which would have been thrown away by East London shops and turns it into three-course meals. The Centre feeds a nutritious meal to an average of 20 people in need a week and has created a genuine community atmosphere.

ABOVE: Doreen Lawrence OBE speaks to the media after carrying the Olympic Flame into the Stephen Lawrence Charitable Trust Centre, Lewisham. She set up the Centre to offer a base for community learning and development following the murder of her teenage son in 1993.

LEFT: Michael Owen, the England striker who began his career at Liverpool, brought the Olympic Flame to Battersea Dogs and Cats Home where 50 canine residents formed a guard of honour.

OPPOSITE: Construction workers line up on scaffolding to applaud the Olympic Torch Relay procession passing by their building site in Hillingdon on Day 67.

ABOVE: An Olympic Rings Flower Display at Kew Gardens provides the stage for young tennis star Oliver Golding's moment to shine. The 18-year-old from Richmond has been the youngest junior British number one tennis player, the 2011 US Open Boys' champion and a Youth Olympic Games gold medallist.

RIGHT: Kathleen Brien, aka Katy B, meets her match in Flame colours. 'I feel like I've been on a bit of a journey with the Torch, getting to know the Olympians and understanding their sacrifices and dedication,' the singer revealed. 'Their mentality is so inspiring.'

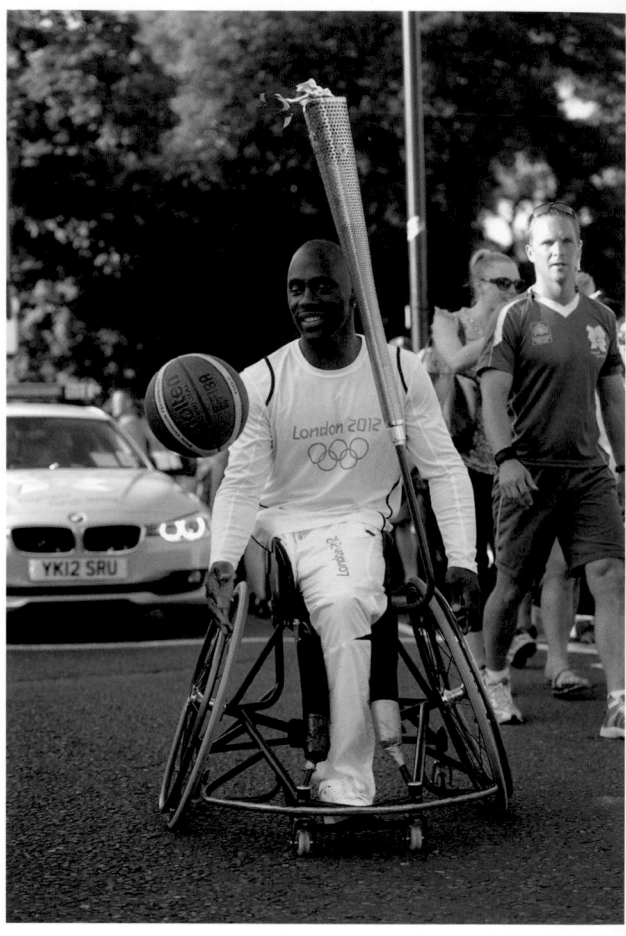

ABOVE: Dhol musicians add to the festivities and thrill crowds in Hounslow with their rhythmical play on the double-headed South Asian drums, which are popular at weddings.

ABOVE RIGHT: Tyler Saunders, a wheelchair basketball athlete on the Lloyds TSB Local Heroes programme, carries the Olympic Flame through Ealing. He was selected because of his commitment, dedication and inspirational qualities.

OPPOSITE: Good service on all lines. John Light, a signalman employed by London Underground, takes the Olympic Flame for a ride on the 7.15am District Line Tube train. The Torch travelled from Wimbledon to Wimbledon Park Station.

'I've worked for London Underground for 49 years ... to hold the Flame is a huge honour for me.'

Signalman and Torchbearer John Light

LEFT: Golden girl. Diana Gould, at 100 years old the oldest female Torchbearer of London 2012, proudly displays the Flame in Barnet on Day 68. Active all her life, she still runs exercise classes at the retirement flats where she lives in northwest London.

RIGHT: A spectator in Brent flies the flag for Team GB and models an impressive torch-style bee-hive – a living demonstration of the Olympic motto of 'faster, higher, stronger'.

BELOW: HRH The Prince of Wales and the Duchess of Cornwall witness the Torch 'kiss' in Haringey between Jay Kamiraz, a beneficiary of the Prince's Trust, and Paralympian athlete Scott Moorhouse.

ABOVE: Olympian Daley Thompson, the first decathlete to hold the World, Olympic, Commonwealth and European titles simultaneously, relishes his approach to the Cauldron for the celebrations at Alexandra Palace. Singer Loick Essien was among the performers in the evening show.

ABOVE RIGHT: Safe pair of hands. Gordon Banks, goalkeeper in England's 1966 World Cup winning football team, retains a commanding presence as he takes the Olympic Flame down Wembley Way, at Wembley Stadium. 'It is a great honour to hold a Torch with a light on it that goes back so many, many, many years,' he said.

'I am very, very proud ... People lining the streets and coming together to celebrate is so evocative of what the Olympic Games stands for.'

Torchbearer Matt Holder who ran through Barnet

ABOVE: Robert Swannell, ambassador for the Team 2012 fundraising appeal, proudly displays the Flame inside the Museum of London. His passion for the Olympic Games was inspired by his grandfather, who competed at the 1924 and 1928 Games.

RIGHT: Ify Egesi, aged 12, receives raucous applause and a horn salute as she holds up the Olympic Flame inside the Globe – or the 'wooden O', as William Shakespeare referred to his theatre.

ABOVE: Enthusiastic applause greets Wheelchair Basketball player Ade Adepitan as he carries the Olympic Flame over the Millennium Bridge in front of St Paul's Cathedral. He was a member of the Great Britain team that won the bronze medal at the 2004 Athens Paralympic Games.

OPPOSITE: Office workers, shoppers and tourists on Oxford Street cheer Saman Jafar, 19, a volunteer coach at Kyu-Yo-Bu-Shin football club in Westminster, as he brandishes the Olympic Flame from the top of an open-top double-decker bus.

Moment to Shine

James Atherton

Inspired by the care and compassion provided by the Yorkshire hospice which was treating his father for cancer, James Atherton resolved to dedicate 2010 to undertaking a fundraising marathon to help support the hospice. He billed it the 10:10:10 – committing himself to ten 10k runs in 2010. He also strong-armed nine of his friends and colleagues to join him in the mission. Over a series of 10 weekends and countless training sessions in-between, James and his crew raised a very fitting £10k which has helped to ensure that the dedicated hospice staff can continue their valuable and selfless work to make the lives of cancer sufferers that little bit easier.

ABOVE RIGHT: Daniel McCubbin, a charity fundraiser and volunteer, holds aloft the Olympic Torch inside St Pancras International Rail Station under the Olympic rings. It marks the exact spot where the London 2012 Torch design, by design company Barber Osgerby, was originally unveiled in June 2011.

'A sea of office workers, families and tourists waving flags, blowing whistles, cheering the Torchbearers along Oxford Street.'

Andy Dangerfield

LEFT: A magnificent spectacle. The Olympic Flame dazzles from a cauldron on the royal barge Gloriana as it passes the iconic Battersea Power Station on Day 70. On the last day of the Torch Relay, it travelled by water from Hampton Court to Tower Bridge.

LEFT: James Cracknell, double gold medallist and endurance challenge addict, is one of many Olympians of all ages to enjoy his turn with an oar on the royal barge.

FAR LEFT: Crowds congregate on leafy river bank stretches and even wade in to glimpse the best views of the Flame as the Gloriana wends her way eastwards down the River Thames.

Moment to Shine

The Final Torchbearers

In the final moments of the Opening Ceremony, seven young British athletes nominated by seven British Olympic heroes became the final Torchbearers, with the honour of lighting the Olympic Cauldron. The young stars were Callum Airlie, 17, a sailor (by Shirley Robertson); Jordan Duckitt, 18, chairman of the London 2012 Young Ambassador Steering Group (by Duncan Goodhew); Desiree Henry, a 16-year-old sprinter (by Daley Thompson); Katie Kirk, 18, a junior European champion pentathlete and runner (Dame Mary Peters); Cameron MacRitchie, a 19-year-old world-class rower (Steve Redgrave); Aidan Reynolds, 18, a javelin thrower (Lynn Davies); and Adelle Tracey, 19, a middle-distance runner (Dame Kelly Holmes).

After Steve Redgrave had passed on the Flame to this new generation, the young athletes took it in turns to carry the Torch around the Stadium. Then each took the Flame to light the magnificent Olympic Cauldron, designed by Thomas Heatherwick.

'We're a warm-up act for the real show coming up.'

Opening Ceremony Director Danny Boyle

OPPOSITE: Journey's end. The Gloriana moors in front of Tower Bridge, sporting its giant Olympic rings, to deliver the Olympic Flame into safekeeping in City Hall prior to the evening's Opening Ceremony.

ABOVE RIGHT: David Beckham thrills the world as he zooms under Tower Bridge on board a speedboat named 'Max Power' to transport the Olympic Torch with its Torchbearer to the Olympic Stadium.

RIGHT: The power and the glory. The Olympic Flame seems to travel at the speed of light on its final journey to the Opening Ceremony on 27 July 2012. When the speedboat, decorated with pink and blue neon lights, reached the Olympic Park, Beckham delivered the Olympic Flame to Great Britain's greatest Olympian, Sir Steve Redgrave.

LEFT: The penultimate Torchbearer. Sir Steve Redgrave, five-time Olympic Rowing gold medallist, walks tall towards seven young athletes, hand-picked by himself and six other British Olympians as potential heroes of the future.

BELOW LEFT: The magnificent seven. Young athletes Callum Airlie, Jordan Duckitt, Desiree Henry, Katie Kirk, Cameron Ritchie, Aidan Reynolds and Adelle Tracey take the Flame on a final run of honour around the athletics track in the closing moments of the Opening Ceremony.

BELOW: The seven GB athletes of the future lean forward in unison to ignite the copper petals that each competing delegation had brought into the Stadium. Each petal bears the country's name and the words 'XXX Olympiad London 2012'.

ABOVE LEFT: The seven lighted copper petals trigger the ignition of all 205 petals, representing each competing nation. Individual flames spread between the petals, which rise up and converge into a cauldron in a stunning single conflagration.

BELOW LEFT: Blazing beauty. The Olympic Cauldron is lit, signalling the opening of sporting competition. Britain's 70-day Torch Relay reaches a fitting climax, celebrating the togetherness of the world under the banner of Olympic values.

OVERLEAF: Spectacular fireworks explode around the roof of the Olympic Stadium, encircling the glorious Olympic Cauldron in a ring of aerial art that could be seen and cheered from miles around.

271

'I declare open the Games of London, celebrating the 30th Olympiad of the modern era.'

HRH Queen Elizabeth II

Week 10 Places

SATURDAY Greenwich • Newham • Tower Hamlets • Hackney • Waltham Forest **SUNDAY** Redbridge • Barking & Dagenham • Havering • Bexley **MONDAY** Lewisham • Bromley • Croydon • Sutton • Merton • Wandsworth **TUESDAY** Kingston • Richmond • Hounslow • Hillingdon • Denham • Ealing **WEDNESDAY** Harrow • Brent • Barnet • Enfield • Haringey **THURSDAY** Camden • Islington • City • Southwark • Lambeth • Wandsworth • Kensington & Chelsea • Hammersmith & Fulham • Westminster **FRIDAY** Hampton Court • Olympic Stadium

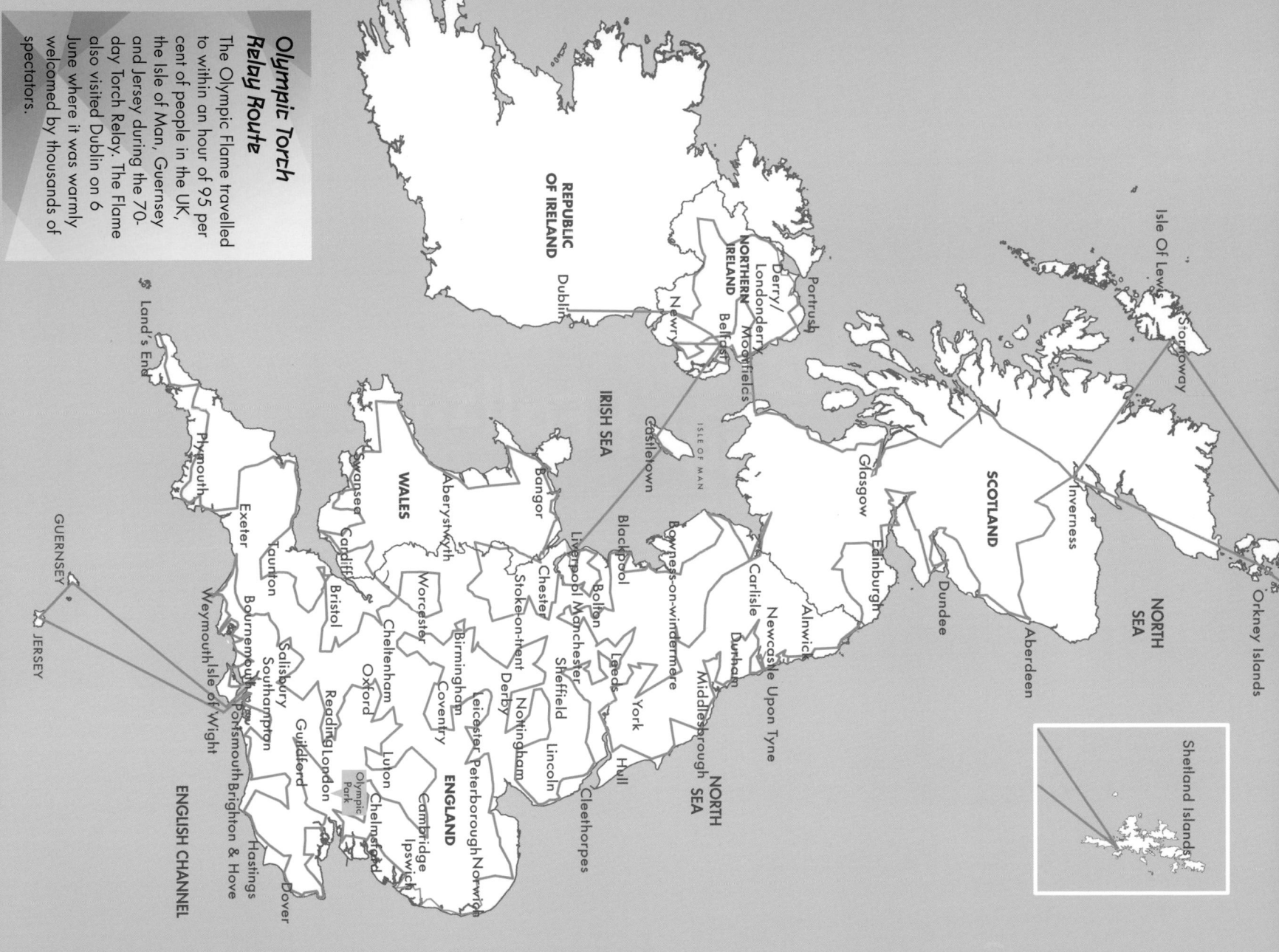

Olympic Torch Relay Route

The Olympic Flame travelled to within an hour of 95 per cent of people in the UK, the Isle of Man, Guernsey and Jersey during the 70-day Torch Relay. The Flame also visited Dublin on 6 June where it was warmly welcomed by thousands of spectators.

REPUBLIC OF IRELAND

Dublin

NORTHERN IRELAND

Derry/Londonderry
Moneyfields
Portrush
Newry
Belfast
Castletown

IRISH SEA

ISLE OF MAN

Isle Of Lewis
Stornoway

Orkney Islands

NORTH SEA

Shetland Islands

SCOTLAND

Inverness
Glasgow
Edinburgh
Dundee
Aberdeen

Alnwick
Newcastle Upon Tyne
Durham
Carlisle
Bowness-on-windermere
Middlesbrough

NORTH SEA

WALES

Aberystwyth
Bangor
Swansea
Cardiff

Chester
Liverpool
Blackpool
Bolton
Manchester
Sheffield
Leeds
York
Hull
Cleethorpes
Lincoln
Nottingham
Derby
Stoke-on-trent
Leicester
Peterborough
Norwich
Coventry
Birmingham
Worcester
Cheltenham

Plymouth
Exeter
Taunton
Bristol

Salisbury
Southampton
Bournemouth
Weymouth
Isle of Wight
Portsmouth
Brighton & Hove
Hastings
Dover

Oxford
Reading
Guildford
London
Olympic Park
Luton
Chelmsford
Cambridge
Ipswich

ENGLAND

GUERNSEY

JERSEY

ENGLISH CHANNEL

Land's End

Chapter 11
As Night Falls...

Highlights

For eight thousand Torchbearers, their 300m stretch was a stage on which to enjoy their moment to shine. The day's final Torchbearer relished the exuberant, often poignant, task of running down the 'Torchbearer corridor' to bring the Olympic Flame into an iconic local gathering point – a city centre square, a beach, a historic field – and ignite the Celebration Cauldron that signalled the finale of one of the 66 evening celebrations across the UK. For local authorities the evening events were a chance to 'take ownership' of the Olympic Flame. They used the symbolic lighting ritual as an open invitation to one and all to come together and party as a community.

From the smallest to the largest, through many historic venues such as Newcastle's Tyne Bridge, Liverpool's Pier Head, Alnwick Castle, Edinburgh Castle, Blackpool Tower Ballroom, Portsmouth's Southsea Common, Singleton Park in Swansea and Belfast's Town Hall to stunning natural settings such as the park at Bowness-on-Windermere and the beach at Weymouth, the stage was set each night for an extraordinary experience that merged big names and local talent, theatrical spectacle with festival mood.

The atmosphere was unique in each location. The first, on the Hoe in Plymouth, resembled a vibrant rock festival; the second, in Exeter, brought family picnickers to the green outside the cathedral. Newry rallied memorably behind the city's final Torchbearer, chanting the name of brave teenage amputee Ryan Cinnamond, as he carried the Torch into Pairc Esler to light the Cauldron. A festive crowd at Cheltenham Racecourse suddenly transformed into a sea of rapt faces as the emotional pairing of Zara Philips and Toytown – the horse that missed out on two Olympic Games due to injury – rode up at a stately pace to do the Cauldron lighting honours.

At Bowness-on-Windermere, the landscape provided a perfect backdrop for 'Lakes Alive: On the Night Shift'. This magnificent combination of firework display and concert sent vivid streams of colour and light through the skies over Lake Windermere, across which the Flame had travelled earlier on the MV Tern. Local indie band British Sea Power and Mercury Prize nominee Katy B were among the performers, and buoyant crowds defied the weather to celebrate an unforgettable event.

The running order of each evening celebration followed a format, with space to feature talented local performance artists. Cameo shows were provided across the UK by street dancers, folk bands, gymnasts, string quartets, choirs, bands, orchestras and ballet dancers. We saw everything – from dance with large inflatable costumes, courtesy of Hull City Council, to 1,000-piece

Red hot vibe: Labrinth, the stage name of rapper Timothy McKenzie, performs a set at the evening celebration at The Amphitheatre in Bristol at the end of Day 4. His star turn was followed by acrobatic and dance performances to welcome the arrival of the Flame.

choirs, an incredible samba band to 120 dancers grooving up the Torchbearer corridor in Lincoln. In Hastings the local organisers wanted the Cauldron ceremony to be enhanced by groups of Morris Dancers in colourful outfits, a large choir dressed in black and dancers in the fiery palette of red, orange and yellows.

Each evening celebration comprised 20 minutes of entertainment from Presenting Partners Samsung (Twist and Pulse street dancers), Lloyds TSB (circus skills based on sport) and Coca-Cola (live music). There was video footage about the Olympic Games and the Olympic Torch Relay, local Olympians with their medals and a charming Children's Promise scene (back in 2004, LOCOG promised children born on 20 December 2004, the date that the bid was submitted, a moment in the limelight). This dovetailed into the arrival of the Flame, with the emotive 'Chariots of Fire' theme signalling a switch in mood. The Master of Ceremonies related the final Torchbearer's inspirational story as he or she came on to the stage, raising the Torch so that the Olympic Flame was visible for all to see, before finally lighting the Celebration Cauldron.

LEFT: Final furlong. Zara Phillips, riding her horse Toytown, shows the Olympic Flame to the 24,000 people thronging Cheltenham Racecourse on the final leg of the Flame's journey on Day 5. 'I'm shaking,' she said after her slot with the Flame. 'It was an unbelievable experience and I am massively honoured for doing it.'

BELOW LEFT: A sea of faces. Crowds are enraptured after an evening celebration of music, dance and circus skills in the presence of the Olympic Flame burning in the Celebration Cauldron in Swansea's Singleton Park.

BELOW: Brit Award winner Emeli Sandé feeds the festival vibe at Coopers Field, a vast green meadow within the picturesque grounds of Cardiff Castle, during an eight-hour city celebration in the Welsh capital.

'It has been absolutely brilliant. It is definitely something I will never, ever forget.'

Torchbearer Lewis Denny, after lighting the Celebration Cauldron for thousands of revellers at Alnwick Castle

LEFT: 'Liverpool, the Olympic Flame is yours…' Craig Lundberg, a war veteran blinded on duty in Iraq in 2007, had the emotive role of final Torchbearer. He took the Flame across the Mersey on board the ferry from Birkenhead before winding through the Torchbearer corridor to light the Cauldron at Pierhead. 'I'm on top of the world,' he grinned, preparing to disembark. 'It's great that I am representing the city – and what an iconic scene.'

ABOVE: Magic touch. Lewis Denny lights the Celebration Cauldron to fire up the evening celebration on Alnwick Castle Pastures. The Castle, home to the Duke and Duchess of Northumberland, was the location for two of the Harry Potter films.

'They all cheer as they see the Flame on the big screen. There's a countdown … Three, two, one … and there it goes!'

Neil Sackley, for BBC Radio Solent

ABOVE: Flame-haired Katy B, the dubstep, R&B, funky, house and UK garage singer-songwriter from London, performs at the evening celebration concert at York Racecourse.

OPPOSITE: A beautiful day. The Torch Relay gave the massed crowds a reason to celebrate as they soak up the rock'n'roll atmosphere under Liverpool's blue skies on Day 14.

ABOVE: Local hero. Jan Booth, County Chairman of Cumbria Young Farmers Clubs, which have 1400 members aged 10 to 26 in 26 clubs around Cumbria, takes the Olympic Flame towards the Cauldron to signal the start of the evening celebration at picturesque Bowness-on-Windermere.

LEFT: A crowd of 10,000 people filled Albert Square in Manchester to watch the lighting of the Celebration Cauldron. Local band The Courteeners finished the party with a rousing set as the rain started to fall.

283

ABOVE: Racing pulses. Overexcited fans scream with admiration for boyband The Wanted, who performed at the evening celebration in Cannon Hill Park, Birmingham. Earlier the boys had carried the Torch through Newton, south Staffordshire.

LEFT: Dancers inspired by circus acts entertain the evening crowd in Meridian Park in Cleethorpes, Lincolnshire, as part of Presenting Partner Lloyds TSB's nightly 20-minute segment on stage.

'Electric atmosphere, fantastic crowd, exceptional emotion and spirit when the Torch came on stage.'

Chris Holmes, describing Birmingham's evening celebration

RIGHT: A jubilant Diana Ludlow stands back after lighting the Celebration Cauldron on Weymouth Beach at the end of Day 55. Her late husband Bill was responsible for the creation of the Weymouth & Portland National Sailing Academy where the London 2012 Olympic and Paralympic Games Sailing events will be held.

BELOW: Iwan Thomas, Olympic sprint medallist, holds up the Olympic Flame to a crowd of 40,000 at the Big Weekend event held on Parkers Piece in Cambridge. He lit the Cauldron and the entertainment continued with community art project 'A Field for Dreams' taking centre stage.

'My heart skipped a beat for a moment there. I couldn't quite believe it and now I'm really looking forward to London 2012.'

Torchbearer Jonathon Bamber, after lighting the Celebration Cauldron on Southsea Common

Index

Abrahams, Harold 15
Ainslie, Ben (first Torchbearer in the UK) 30, *32*, 33
Angel of the North 134
aquarium, Hull *141*
art installations *see* sculptures and art installations
Aysgarth Falls 143, *143*

Barber, Edward (of Barber Osgerby, Olympic and Paralympic Torch designers) 8, 22–3, 266
Bath 28–9, 43
Belfast 82, *87*, 95, 96
Berlin 1936 Games, first Torch Relay 8
Brands Hatch *245*
bridges: Bridge of Sighs, Cambridge 209; Clifton Suspension Bridge, Bristol *46*; Humber Bridge, Hull 140; Millennium Bridge, London 264; packhorse bridge, Carrbridge 115; rope bridge, Carrick-a-Rede 83, 91; Sail Bridge, Swansea *61*; Samuel Beckett Bridge, Dublin *97*; Tower Bridge, London 229, *245*, 268, 269; Transporter Bridge, Middlesbrough 139; Tyne Bridge, Newcastle 126, *128*
Brighton 246
Bullfinch (designers of Torch burner system) 25

Callanish Standing Stones, Isle of Lewis *104–5*, *114*
Cambridge 209; Great Court Run 208

Cardiff *52*, 53, *61*
Carrick-a-Rede 91
castles: Alnwick *122*; Beaumaris 69; Caerphilly *61*; Carrickfergus 88; Conisbrough *176*; Dover 240; Dunluce 89; Dunster 40; Kendal *148*; Norwich *196*, 200; Oystermouth 63; Richmond *145*; Tonbridge 238; Urquhart *108*; Warkworth *125*; Warwick *187*; Windsor *11*, *213*
cathedrals: Durham 137; Lincoln *172*; St Magnus, Kirkwall (Orkney) *113*; Peterborough *190*; St Paul's (London) *264*; Salisbury *221*; Wells *42*, *54*; Winchester *219*
Cauldron (Olympic Cauldron) 27, 53, *77*, *132*, *271*; lighting 47, 58, 59, 73, 74, 78, 107, 108, *141*, 157, 173, 180, 190, 204, 228; London 1948 Games 14–15; at Paralympic Games 26
Ceredigion Cob Horse *65*
'Chariots of Fire' 47, 107, *118*, *118*, 209
cliffs: Durdle Door *224*; Seven Sisters 237
Coe, Lord (Sebastian), Chair of LOCOG 156, *165*, *214*, *245*
Crosby Beach 76

Dartmouth, Royal Naval College 36, *37*
Deighton, Paul (LOCOG Chief Executive) 84
Dockyard, Portsmouth Historic *233*

Doran, Stephen (Senior Operations Manager, LOCOG) 16
Dublin 82–83, *95–97*

Eden Project 31
Edinburgh 106, *119*, *120*, *121*

Falkirk Wheel 121
'Firefly', The, BA2012 16, *27*, 34, 82, *84*, *113*, 228, 234
football stadia 161, *188*, 235
Fountains Abbey 152
Foxton Locks *181*, *188*

gallery *see* museums and galleries
Gateshead 134, *136*
Gianniotis, Spyros (first Torchbearer in Greece) 9
Giant's Causeway 90
Glastonbury Tor *45*
Gormley, Anthony, sculptures 58, *76*, *134*, 144
Grimsby, The Royal Dock Tower *157*, *171*, *171*
Guru Nanak Marg Gundwara (Sikh temple, Gravesend) 244
Guernsey 228, 234

Hadrian's Wall *135*
Hartlepool *138*
Heatherwick, Thomas (designer of Olympic Cauldron) 268
Hull 140, *141*
Isle of Lewis *104–5*, 106, *114*, 115
Isle of Man 16, 17, 82, 84–5, *86*, 100, 102

Isle of Wight 228, 230, *230*
itinerary of London 2012 Torch Relay 15–17, 26–7, 30, 55, 79, 103, 129, 153, 177, 201, 225, 247, 274, 275; final Torchbearers (in the Opening Ceremony) 268, 270; start of 27

John O'Groats *111*
Jersey 228

Kew Gardens 259
'kisses' (Torch 'kisses', passing on the Flame) 33, 35, 37, 67, 83, 91, 160, 181, 193, 195, 232, 262

Lake Windermere 148
landmarks featured 53, 72, 91, 95, 95, 121, 134, 143, *143*, 148, 171, 175, 229, 230, 245
Land's End 30, *32*, 33
Lavers, Ralph (Torch designer for 1948 Games) 9–10
Laxey Wheel, Isle of Man 102
Liverpool 59, *77*, 78
LOCOG nomination process 24
London 1948 Games ('Austerity Games') 9; final Torchbearer (John Mark) 14–15; Lighting Ceremony 8, 10; Opening Ceremony 14–15; Torch design 9–10; *see also* 'Relay of Peace'
London 2012 Games; Lighting Ceremony 8, 9; Opening Ceremony 251, 270, 271; Torch's arrival 245

London Eye 256

Margate 242, 243
Mark, John (final Torchbearer for 1948 Games) 14–15, *15*
modes of transport 17; other Host Nations 17, *17*; abseil *134*, 157, 171, 200, 229, 245; air: helicopter 30, *32*, 229; plane 27, *84*, 113, 234; balloon 31; bikes: BMX bike 162; motorbike 84; motorcycle sidecar 17; mountain bike 109, 245; quadbike 115; unicycle 93; boats: 98, 108, 110, 121; canal boat 42, 72, 73; coxed rowing boat 89; electric-powered 42; ferries 59, 77, 197, 231; Fire Brigade boat 257; lifeboats 59, 69, 85, 226–7; Norwegian longboat 112; powerboat 33; punt 209; rowing boats 89, 213; royal barge (Gloriana) 244, 267, 268; sailing boat 255; speedboat 269; steamboat 148; tall ships 226–7; warship 138; white-water raft 206; yacht 195; cable cars: 175; chairlift 230; skilift gondola 111; horseback: 33, 47, 65, 69, 86 (horse tram), 141, 205; cob horse 65; jet pack 190; rail: Barking Park miniature railway 255; Cleethorpes Coast Light Railway 166; District Line Tube train 261; Ffestiniog Railway 67; Great Central Railway

190; Manx Electric Railway 86; mountain railway 56–7; Nene Valley Railway 191; Severn Valley Railway 50; steam trains 50, 139, 144, 166; Swansea Bay Rider 64 trams 86, 150, 182; zip wire 126

Moment to Shine: Allen, June and Frank 37; Anderton, Jordan 35; Atherton, James 266; Bannister, Sir Roger 15, 215; Bassloe, Arthur 124; Bingham, Andrea 96; Bonington, Sir Chris 68; Brown, Morna 112; Burns, Vanessa 239; Comaneci, Nadia 254; Coogan, Andy 117; Dale-Beeton, Emily 86; Davies, Elin 66; Deary, Terry 145; Easter, Melanie 187; Final Torchbearers 268; Forselles, Bernard Af 241; Fox, Ben 46, 47; Hill, Tony 40; Littlewood, Robert 161; Lusted, Jay 70; Mitchell, Jack 165; Murray, Karen 194; Oliver, Jamie 208; Parkinson, Ben 168; Passmore, Gemma 51; Peake, John 191; Phillips, Zara, HRH, 48, 48; Regan, Eleanore 44; Richard, Sir Cliff 184; Rothband, Mia 136; Salmon, Zoe 98; Smith, Matt 60; Stokes, Kay 138; Thornton, Ryan 158; Traill, Tom 267; Watson, Kylie 88; Weedon, George 218

Mount Snowdon 68

Much Wenlock 58–9, 71, 73

museums and galleries: Black Country Living Museum 182; Bletchley Park 210; Imperial War Museum,

Duxford 207; Museum of London 264; National Coal Mining Museum, Wakefield 163; National Museum of Wales 51; Tall Ships Museum, Glasgow 110; Turner Contemporary Gallery, Margate 243

Nation and Regions Group (LOCOG) 15–16

National Library of Wales, Aberystwyth 66

National Memorial Arboretum 183

North Greenwich Arena 254

Northern Ireland 16, 82-83, 83, 87, 88–95, 96, 98–9

Northumberland 19

Olympic Cauldron see Cauldron

Olympic Stadium 8, 9, 272–3

Olympic Torches 20–1

Omagh 93

Orkney Islands 16, 111, 112, 113

Osgerby, Jay (of Barber Osgerby, Olympic and Paralympic Torch designers) 8, 22–3, 24, 266

Paralympic Relay 25–6

parks: Fairlop Waters Country Park 255; Lynnsport and Leisure Park 192; Marble Arch Caves Global Geopark 94; Needles Park and Chairlift, Isle of Wight 230; North York Moors National Park 144; Pembrokeshire Coast National Park 58; sculpture parks 164, 236, see

also zoos and safari parks

Police Torch Security Team see Torch Security Team

Pontcysyllte Aqueduct 72

Portsmouth 233, 234

Premier Group, Coventry (Olympic Torch manufacturer) 23, 24, 24

racecourses 30, 47, 58, 69, 75, 141, 205

Redgrave, Sir Steve 216, 268, 269, 270

'Relay of Peace' (London 1948 Games) 10, 11–13, 11, 12, 14–16, 15

Richards, Mark (logistics manager, Torch Relay) 18

Royal Family: HRH Queen Elizabeth II 14, 214, 272; HRH The Duke of Edinburgh 14, 214; HRH The Prince of Wales (Prince Charles) 262; HRH The Duchess of Cornwall 262; HRH The Duke of Cambridge 250; HRH The Duchess of Cambridge 250; HRH Prince Harry 250; HRH the Princess Royal (Princess Anne) 27, 47; HRH Princess Beatrice of York 132; George VI 9, 14; HRH Queen Elizabeth the Queen Mother 15

Royal Pavilion, Brighton 246

safari parks see zoos and safari parks

St Michael's Mount 33

St Pancras International Rail Station 266

Scholey, Mark (programme manager

for Torch Relay) 23, 25

sculptures and art installations 76, 89, 134, 165, 236, 243

Scotland 16, 83, 100–101, 106–107, 120–121, 123

Shetland Islands 16, 106, 112

Spinnaker Tower, Portsmouth 233

stadia 9, 96, 136, 161, 166, 188, 215, 231, 235, 263, 272–3

standing stones 104–5, 114, 202–3, 220

stately homes: Blenheim Palace 211; Chatsworth 175; Christchurch Mansion 199; Hall Place 255; Hatfield House 209; Hopetoun House 119; Newstead Abbey 175; Petworth House 236; Temple Newsam, Leeds 162

statues 59, 116, 151, 189

steam locomotives 139, 144 see also modes of transport

Stonehenge 202–3, 220

Stormont 87

Stratford-upon-Avon 186

Tecosim (product engineers) 23

theatres: Globe Theatre 264; Scarborough Open Air Theatre 140

Torch design 8, 22–3, 24, 25; for Paralympic Torch Relay 25–6

Torch Relay: history 8–9, 17; itinerary see itinerary; logistics 17–19; other Host Nations 17

Torch Security Team 34, 42, 51, 67, 94, 126, 207, 231, 234, 242

Torchbearers: final Torchbearer of 1948 Relay 14-15, 15; final Torchbearers of London 2012 Relay 268, 270; first Torchbearers of London 2012 Relay 9, 30, 32, 33; selection of for London 2012 Relay 16, 22

Torches: all Games from 1936 20–1, 25; varied designs 25

Torvill and Dean 172

Tower of London 229, 245

Wales 16, 51, 52, 53, 58, 60–70

Western Isles 16, 104–105, 106, 114–115

Wembley Stadium 263

Williams, Simon (organiser, Torch Relay) 18–19

Wooderson, Sydney 14, 15

York 141

zoos and safari parks 33, 50, 58, 76, 87

Chapter Opener Captions

Chapter 1: The Royal Crescent, Bath, a Grade I listed Georgian architectural delight, provides a stunning backdrop as picnickers, families and sun-worshippers in Royal Victoria Park await the arrival of the Olympic Flame.

Chapter 2: Full steam ahead! The Snowdon Mountain Railway carries the Olympic Flame up the steep slope of the highest mountain in Wales. Legendary mountaineer Sir Chris Bonington was given the honour of carrying the Flame to the summit, as he scaled the peak he first conquered 61 years ago.

Chapter 3: Torchbearer Peter Jack holds the Olympic Flame aloft on Giant's Causeway during Day 17 of the Torch Relay. The UNESCO World Heritage Site is made up of 40,000 large black basalt hexagonal columns protruding from the sea.

Chapter 4: A lone piper plays as Commonwealth gold medallist Kirsty Wade holds the Olympic Flame as the sun rises at the Callanish Standing Stones, dating from 3000 BC, on the Isle of Lewis.

Chapter 5: A flotilla joins Stephanie Booth, who stands on board the steamboat Tern, as she carries the Olympic Flame across Lake Windermere to a spectacular firework and dance party in Bowness-on-Windermere.

Chapter 6: In the Red Hall of the MAGNA Science Adventure Centre in Yorkshire, Debjani Chatterjee holds the Olympic Torch. The indoor centre celebrates the four elements of Air, Earth, Fire and Water.

Chapter 7: Beside the seaside. Caroline Emeny, village stalwart and cancer survivor, parades the Olympic Torch in front of Southwold's famous, brightly painted beach huts. The huts give a cheerful summer resonance to this historic town on the Suffolk coast.

Chapter 8: Relay star. Michael Johnson stands with the Flame at dawn in front of the prehistoric standing stones of Stonehenge. The American, 44, won four Olympic gold medals, and still holds the world and Olympic Games records in the 400m and 4 x 400m Relay.

Chapter 9: On the high seas. The Olympic Flame is delivered by a RNLI rescue boat from Samphire Hoe to the brig-rigged Stavros S Niarchos – which is owned by the Tall Ships Youth Trust and provides personal development voyages for young people – ready for transportation to the Prince of Wales pier in Dover.

Chapter 10: On top of the world. Amelia Hempleman-Adams poses with the Olympic Flame on the roof of a London Eye pod. 'The height was quite scary, but it was a once in a lifetime experience, especially as the Olympic Games are in London,' said the 17-year-old who last year became the youngest person to ski to the South Pole.

Chapter 11: Strictly Come Celebrating. Harry Judd, the drummer from McFly, and Aliona Vilani, the professional dancer with whom he won the BBC dance programme, waltz across the Blackpool Tower ballroom floor to light the Celebration Cauldron. Heavy rain and high winds forced the evening celebration inside from its proposed site on the Tower Festival headland.

Acknowledgements

Cover images: all © Press Association for LOCOG

The Publisher would like to thank the Press Association for the use of their images:

© Ben Birchall (Press Association for LOCOG): pp. 28-29, p. 31, p. 33 (top), p. 38 (top left, top right), p. 39, p. 42, p. 45, p. 46 (both), p. 47, p. 50 (all), p. 51 (right), p. 62 (right), p. 83, p. 88 (both), p. 94, p. 95, p. 98 (top left), p. 100 (left), p. 111 (below), p. 112 (both), p. 113 (both), p. 115 (top), pp. 130-131, p. 137 (left), p. 137 (below), p. 140 (top left, below), p. 143 (right), p. 144 (below), p. 147 (left), p. 150 (top, below), p. 151 (left), p. 158 (top), p. 162 (right), p. 163 (top, right), p. 164, p. 165 (below), pp. 178-179, p. 181, p. 188 (both), p. 191 (left), p. 192, p. 193 (below), p. 194, p. 195 (right), p. 198 (right), p. 209 (left, right), p. 210 (left), p. 244 (left), p. 252 (right), p. 253, p. 255 (top), p. 257 (both), p. 258 (left), p. 259 (below, right), p. 260 (right), p. 263 (right), p. 267 (top), p. 283 (below), p. 285 (left). **© Gareth Fuller (Press Association for LOCOG):** p. 53, p. 59, p. 60, p. 61 (top left), p. 65, p. 66 (both), p. 69 (below), p. 72, p. 74 (top left, top right), p. 76 (left, top right), p. 78, p. 101, p. 110, p. 111 (top), p. 116 (left), p. 121 (left), p. 122, p. 123 (right), p. 125 (right), p. 126 (left), p. 134 (top), p. 136 (both), p. 157, p. 160 (top, below), p. 161 (below), p. 166 (both), p. 168, p. 170 (left), p. 172 (both), p. 173, p. 175 (right), p. 182 (left), p. 184, p. 187 (top), p. 195 (left), pp. 203-204, p. 205, p. 213 (top), p. 215 (left), p. 217, p. 219 (left), p. 221 (left, top), p. 222 (top right), p. 222 (below right), p. 229, p. 232 (right), p. 234 (top), p. 235 (right), p. 236 (below), p. 254, p. 258 (right), p. 261, p. 262 (top, right), p. 264 (below), p. 266, p. 268, p. 282, p. 285 (right). **© Joe Giddens (Press Association for LOCOG):** p. 2, p. 7, p. 41 (left, bottom right), p. 51 (left), p. 53 (below), p. 54, p. 61 (bottom left, right), p. 62 (left), p. 64 (right), p. 67 (top right, below), p. 68, p. 69 (right), p. 143 (top), p. 145 (left), p. 146 (below), p. 148 (left), p. 150 (left), p. 151 (right), p. 158 (below), p. 159, p. 160 (right), p. 161 (top), p. 162 (left), p. 163 (below), p. 165 (top), p. 167 (left), p. 169, p. 171 (below), p. 176, 213 (below), p. 215 (right), p. 239 (below), p. 240 (left, below), p. 241, p. 242 (right, below), p. 244 (right), p. 256, p. 259 (top), pp. 276-277, p. 279, p. 280 (left, right), p. 283 (top). **© Danny Lawson (Press Association for LOCOG):** p. 92 (both), p. 97, p. 98 (bottom left), pp. 104-105, p. 108 (all), p. 109, p. 111 (left), p. 114 (both), p. 115 (left, below), p. 116 (right), p. 119 (both), p. 120 (left),

p. 196 (both), p. 197, p. 198 (left), p. 199 (right), p. 207 (left), p. 208 (right), p. 209 (top), p. 210 (right), p. 211, p. 212 (right), p. 218, p. 219 (top), p. 220, p. 221 (below), p. 222 (left). **© Yui Mok (Press Association for LOCOG):** p. 34 (both), p. 35 (both), p. 38 (below), p. 40 (right), p. 41 (top right), p. 43 (both), p. 44, p. 48, p. 74 (below), p. 75, p. 76 (below), p. 77 (below), p. 84 (left), p. 86 (both), p. 87 (right), p. 89 (below), p. 90, p. 91 (both), p. 93 (both), p. 96 (both), p. 98 (right), p. 99 (both), p. 123 (top), p. 124 (both), p. 127, p. 133, p. 134 (below), p. 137 (top), p. 138 (below), p. 139 (both), p. 141 (left), p. 144 (top), p. 145 (below), p. 146 (top, left), p. 147 (right), p. 149, p. 152, p. 174 (both), p. 183 (both), p. 185, p. 186, p. 187 (below), p. 189 (both), p. 190 (left, below), p. 193 (top), p. 199 (left), p. 200, p. 207 (right), p. 208 (left), pp. 226-227, p. 229, p. 230, p. 231 (left), p. 233, p. 234 (below), p. 236 (right), p. 238, p. 239 (top), p. 240 (right), p. 243 (right), p. 245 (both), p. 246, p. 252 (left), p. 255 (below), p. 262 (below), p. 263 (left), p. 264 (top), p. 267 (below left, below right), p. 280 (top), p. 281 (right), p. 283 (left), p. 284 (right). **© Chris Radburn (Press Association for LOCOG):** p. 33 (below), p. 36, p. 37 (both), p. 63, p. 64 (left), p. 67 (top left), p. 69 (top), p. 70 (both), p. 71 (both), p. 73 (both), p. 77 (top), p. 84 (top, below), p. 85, p. 87 (left), p. 102, p. 107, p. 117 (both), p. 118, p. 120 (right), p. 121 (right), p. 125 (left), p. 126 (right), p. 135, p. 138 (top), p. 140 (top right), p. 141 (top, below), pp. 154-155, p. 167 (right), p. 170 (right), p. 171 (top), p. 175 (left), p. 182 (right), p. 190 (top), p. 191 (right), p. 212 (left), p. 214, p. 216, p. 219 (right), p. 223, p. 231 (right), p. 232 (left), p. 234 (right), p. 235 (left), p. 236 (top), p. 237, p. 242 (left), p. 243 (left), p. 255 (left), p. 260 (left), p. 264 (right), p. 265, p. 281 (left), p. 284 (left). **© Lewis Whyld (Press Association for LOCOG):** pp. 248-249.

Other images courtesy of: p. 4: © Barber Osgerby; p. 9: © 2012 Getty Images; p. 11: both © Hulton Archive/Getty Images; p. 12: © Hulton Archive/Getty Images; p. 15: © Hulton Archive/Getty Images; p. 17: © Getty Images; pp. 20-21: © 2011 International Olympic Committee; p. 24: all © LOCOG; p. 27: © Getty Images; p. 32: © 2012 Getty Images; p. 40: top left © 2012 Getty Images; pp. 56-57: © 2012 Getty Images; pp. 80-81: © LOCOG; p. 89: © 2012 Getty Images; p. 100: right © 2012 Getty Images; p. 128: © 2012 Getty Images; p. 148: right © 2012 Getty Images, p. 206: © 2012 Getty Images; p. 269: both © Getty Images; pp. 270-273: all © AFP/Getty Images.